WHAT PEOPLE ARE SAYING ABOUT

THE HUMAN RIGHTS MANIFESTO

Like all great manifestos, this one not only dazzles with the sheer
brilliance of its diagnosis of the contemporary world; it also gives us
a new moral vocabulary in which to phrase our aspirations for
political and economic change. And it is no accident that it should
appear as, starting with the Green Movement in Iran and the Arab
Spring, a new politics of dignity becomes visible around the world.
Everyone should read it.
Pankaj Mishra, essayist and novelist.

In her well-argued Manifesto Julie Wark puts neoliberalism and the
ruling elite of the neoliberal democracies of the West on trial. She
asserts that the neoliberal system is intrinsically inimical to human
rights. She supports this radical assertion with well-researched
evidence. Rights, she says, are the basis of dignity, freedom and
justice; without them no human being can be free. Neoliberalism is a
rogue system that cherishes the non-human value of money instead
of human values. She explains the political economy of neoliberalism
in succinct and lucid terms that are not clouded by jargon, making
this document a joy to read. Backed by grim statistics she argues that
the present global order is a crime against humanity. She traces
various crimes against the human race through various historical
epochs to the present. She illustrates cogently how the atrocities of,
for instance, the Khmer Rouge and of blood-thirsty African militias
in the Congo and in other theatres of conflict, are in fact the crimes of
neoliberalism. She portrays neoliberalism as an insidious system that
promotes new forms of slavery, human trafficking and child labor
She makes the chilling observation
enslaved today than they were at th
trade on which the wealth of nations
of today's slaves are women and chil

tarianism are the empire's neoliberal tool of conquest, subjugation and exploitation. Indeed, humanitarianism is a vehicle of Western hegemony. She denounces world governments and corporations as the criminals, but citizens who are enjoying the benefits of these policies and are indifferent to the plight of the rest of the world are not absolved. They are accomplices. And finally she defines what genuine human rights should be. The solutions that she proposes, to begin the world all over again involving what she calls the commoning, the human rights republic, and the universalizing of property, are quite radical, to say the least. These concepts, of course, need further development. This Manifesto would be a great companion for civil society organizations and individual activists. It should be required reading for both non-governmental and government agencies.

Zakes Mda, eminent South African novelist, poet, painter and playwright, whose most recent work is the highly acclaimed memoir *Sometimes There Is a Void*

A Port Huron Statement for the Occupy Generation with a breath-taking vision of planting 'human rights republics' in the practices of daily life.

Mike Davis

Article 1 of the Universal Declaration of Human Rights declares 'All human beings are born free and equal in dignity and rights.' Yet half the world's population lives in extreme poverty without the conditions for freedom or dignity and with very few if any rights. Julie Wark's *Human Rights Manifesto* is vivid, clear and passionate. Her case against neo-liberalism and her case for basic income is an appeal to common sense and a call to action.

Peter Cochrane, historian

Julie Wark's manifesto is a call to action. It asks that you and I as global citizens insist that EVERYONE has the basic human rights that deliver not only freedom, justice and self-determination, but also individual dignity. Only a heartless person could read this and not feel an instant compulsion to act.

Dr Anita Heiss, Aboriginal Australian academic, author and activist

Many states have committed appalling crimes in the name of human rights. Julie Wark provides a great deal of material demonstrating this. She also very convincingly argues that the most basic human right is that of the guaranteed material existence of every member of society. Now, in 2012, when governments are engaged in a full-blown offensive against the conditions of existence of their populations, Wark's defence of universal human rights in this Manifesto is admirable for its intellectual courage.

Daniel Raventós (University of Barcelona and President of Basic Income Network of Spain)

With this Manifesto, Julie Wark has provided an extraordinary and important contribution to the literature on human rights. With great passion and eloquence, she expands the concept of human rights to encompass economic justice for all – the great animating principle of the Arab Spring and the Occupy movement. While not everyone will agree with this formulation, it is impossible to deny the power of her reasoning.

Michael Klare, Five College Professor of Peace and World Security Studies, Hampshire College

The
Human Rights
Manifesto

The
Human Rights
Manifesto

Julie Wark

Winchester, UK
Washington, USA

First published by Zero Books, 2013
Zero Books is an imprint of John Hunt Publishing Ltd., Laurel House, Station Approach,
Alresford, Hants, SO24 9JH, UK
office1@jhpbooks.net
www.johnhuntpublishing.com
www.zero-books.net

For distributor details and how to order please visit the 'Ordering' section on our website.

ISBN: 978 1 78099 666 0

A CIP catalogue record for this book is available from the British Library.

Design: Stuart Davies

Printed and bound by CPI Group (UK) Ltd, Croydon, CR0 4YY

We operate a distinctive and ethical publishing philosophy in all
areas of our business, from our global network of authors to
production and worldwide distribution.

CONTENTS

Introduction

A great number of people have forged the words of this Manifesto for its concerns are as old and all-embracing as humanity itself: freedom, justice and human dignity. It is neither a treatise nor yet another declaration or list of human rights. Its author is an ordinary citizen who has lived long enough to see with horror and indignation how the human rights of the great majority of the world's people have been systematically crushed or, in many cases, literally bulldozed away because they are deemed to be an obstacle to the material interests of a relatively very small number of their fellow humans. This Manifesto is a legitimate claim to all the rights that are still enshrined in many declarations, a demand for rights that have been promised to all of humanity, and a denunciation of promises that have not been kept and of the violations that occur every second of every day on this planet. These are *human* rights and "human" is a universal category. It makes no sense to speak of "human rights" unless they are universal. If rights are limited to only some members of society and denied to others, then we are talking about privileges. And privileges are defended tooth and nail by politicians, rich individuals and enterprises that shamelessly claim, whenever possible, to be defending "human rights", which now tends to be a grandiloquent doublespeak term bound with such abstractions as national "security" or, in other cases, unchecked "rights" for some people who do not recognise that human rights entail duties *vis-à-vis* the rest.

If they are to have any real meaning, human rights must be extracted from naïve and cynical discourse and situated where they belong, in the realm of political economy, part of the bedrock of a well-functioning society. Human beings need to live in society and this essential, universal social condition logically implies that the basic right of material existence should be met for every member of any society. Otherwise, some beings in the society would be reduced to a subhuman condition. All other rights and, in particular, human dignity follow from this. This Manifesto not only argues that an ethical approach to political economy – recognising the right to freedom, justice and human dignity of all human beings – is essential for implementing and guaranteeing human rights but that protection of human rights is also essential for a global economy that works as an "economy" should, in the original sense of properly managing resources.

For far too long we have been fed the story that "civilisation" is to be measured by sustained "improvement" (whatever that means) in the material quality of life. The missing part of this story is that this improvement is only enjoyed by a few people who live in boundless, unregulated abundance, and is paid for by the hunger, hardship and lives of many others. The material upshot of this materialist "civilisation" is a world in which 17 per cent of the population consumes 80 per cent of its resources, 358 billionaires have assets exceeding the combined annual incomes of countries that account for 45 percent of the global population, and one in seven people go hungry. There are many other statistics showing this fast-increasing disparity. This is not "progress" but a shrinking circle of privilege. It belies the values the West claims to uphold and, in this ethical absence, it is bad economics since, by nurturing the very uncivilised greed and lying that govern our economic systems today, it has demon-strably led to the generalised hardship of today's "crisis" and befuddlement (or dishonesty) among experts who are supposed to be finding a way out of it. It is evident that something is very wrong with the system. Not too many decades ago, when people wanted to refer to the probity of any institution, they used the non-ironic simile "as safe as the Bank of England". Nowadays, "banks" engage in serious criminal activity and get bailed out by governments, which are destroying social welfare systems, leaving the population stranded in all kinds of hardship, in the name of rescuing "banks". A totally sociopathic system has been imposed on the vast majority of human beings who would just like to live a decent life in harmony with their fellows.

Although the Universal Declaration of Human Rights was ratified in the General Assembly of the United Nations on 10 December 1948 with forty-eight votes in favour, none against and only eight abstentions,[1] this worldwide endorsement of human rights has amounted to very little in real terms. Poverty statistics vary considerably, which is a clear enough sign in itself that human rights are not taken seriously by the global and national institutions that are supposed to be upholding them. Yet it's worse than that. When estimates consistently suggest that about fifty per cent of the world's population lives in poverty (on less than the rather arbitrary figure of $2.50 per day) – which means that some three and a half billion people are not able to enjoy even the most basic rights because a person living in poverty can't live in conditions of freedom and dignity, let alone justice – we can only conclude that the words "human rights" in the mouths of politicians are no more than cynical mummery. The gap between rich and poor keeps growing ever-faster and, moreover, apart from the colossal injustice, it is difficult to see anything dignified in a perversely clownish life of aimless luxury consumption, a string of vast homes and fleets of cars and private jets. Rather, it confirms Wittgenstein's observation that "Ethics and aesthetics are one".

The key to righting this cruel situation lies in a radical claim, a clamour for the rights that are legally recognised as being the natural inheritance of every single human being, rights that are inseparable from human dignity, the freedom and equality that this entails, and the fraternity that can't exist without them. This Manifesto is an appeal for people from all walks of life to claim the rights that constitute the essence of a truly human existence because, as Article 1 of the Universal Declaration of Human Rights states, "All human beings are born free and equal in

3

dignity and rights. They are endowed with reason and conscience and should act toward one another in a spirit of brotherhood".[2] This means that everybody must recognise and respect our common humanity and, in particular, the fact that, in social life, rights and duties are inseparable so my rights can't undermine your rights, and billionaires should not be swanking about in private jets at the expense of the rights of anybody, let alone those of millions upon millions of people. We need political mechanisms and institutions to be set in place as the product of human "reason and conscience" in order to protect everybody's rights from the abuses of those who want too much. Greed is an ugly thing. Wherever it flourishes it kills the spirit of brotherhood, sisterhood and shared humanity. It has its own Decalogue: 1) My God is Mammon; 2) I bow only before the images of money, palaces, yachts and private jets, am jealous of all who have more than me, and my iniquity shall be passed on to my children; 3) My name shall not be taken in vain for the laws of the rich protect me; 4) My servants, everywhere in the world, shall have no day of rest but shall labour for me twelve hours a day, every day of the year; 5) I shall, if it suits me, sell not only my grandmother but my father, mother, children, sisters and brothers too, and enslave everyone else's; 6) I shall kill people for money (they are faraway and unimportant); 7) Adultery is very profitable if you are a human trafficker; 8) I shall dispossess as many people as possible; 9) I shall bear false witness against anyone if there is money in it; 10) I covet everything my neighbour owns and all the houses, land, oil and servants in the world.

"Universal" is often derided as a utopian, starry-eyed notion when coupled with the word "rights" but it is also revolutionary, precisely because there are always people who want much more than their share of power, wealth and privileges, invariably at the expense of others. The less respect rulers have for rights, the more vicious are their attacks on those who claim them. Anybody who protests at their abuse of power, their greed and its twin sibling cruelty is a troublemaker, a renegade, a traitor, or a subversive and is thus submitted to laws that have little to do with justice. The enemies of human rights will turn to any form of brutality in order to preserve the spoils of their greed, which by some insane, delirious logic, they take as their due. In a perverse way, their savagery attests to the power of human rights.

On 17 December 2010, Mohamed Bouazizi, a street vendor of the Tunisian town of Sidi Bouzid, set himself on fire after repeated harassment by local authorities. Mohamed Bouazizi, a man who was not allowed to live a dignified existence, made his claim by means of a resounding protest at being deprived of his rights, a despairing act that shocked thousands of other people in the Arab world and then inspired them to claim human rights and dignity for themselves and everybody else. His voice rings out in this Manifesto. Bouazizi immolated himself in the final declaration of a man who had been stripped of his freedom and dignity and whose right to material existence was in jeopardy. His action was one of despair resulting in a horrific, tragic death that deprived an already-deprived family of a valued member. This Manifesto is a response to Mohamed Bouazizi's sacrifice because, when he drew attention in this way to the outrage of being stripped of his rights, he was speaking for billions of people. If his cry for universal human rights goes unheeded, we are all in danger of losing our humanity.

Mohamed Bouazizi was a victim of small-town Tunisian authorities, people he knew. Most victims of human rights abuse never see those who cause their torment for they inhabit offices on the other side of the world. At least 250,000 poor farmers in India are said to have committed suicide in the past sixteen years but the figure would seem to be significantly under-reported as women are not deemed to be farmers. They have been driven to kill themselves by high-salaried executives in natty suits. After India was pushed by the World Trade Organisation into adopting seed patenting and thus allowing the huge agribusiness Monsanto to monopolise the market, poor farmers were inveigled by promises of high yields and material benefits to grow the company's Bt cotton and other crops which require an expensive regime of pesticides and fertilisers. They soon became heavily indebted and, with no hope of repaying their debt, killed themselves, often by drinking the Monsanto pesticide they couldn't afford. In Europe, too, official crisis-related – bank-related, rating-agency-related – suicide figures have spiked sharply, up 24 per cent in Greece, more than 16 per cent in Ireland, and 52 percent in Italy.[3] Wherever they are, many of the people who are taking their lives clearly understand what human dignity should be and they prefer to die because a life without dignity isn't worth living.

Human rights are about life, a free and dignified life for everyone. They may have been sequestered, watered down, denied and abused over history. They are not charity. They are not something to be capriciously or grudgingly doled out by the powers-that-be. They are a legitimate claim, a claim that must be made on a global scale. If they are not for everybody, they are not right.

As history's most rousing Manifesto[4] once warned, "a spectre is haunting" the world, the spectre of human dignity. Mohamed Bouazizi's suicide sparked a country-wide series of protests and riots over long-festering social and political grievances because the majority of the population of Tunisia was all too well acquainted his plight. The flames of his despair became a blaze of anger and courageous resolve that burned brightly after his death on 4 January and eventually forced the autocratic President Zine El Abidine Ben Ali – said to have amassed a personal fortune of some $US 5.7 billion – to flee ten days later. The "volcano of rage" spread rapidly through the Arab world. Other people set themselves alight and the people of Egypt, Libya, Algeria, Bahrain, Djibouti, Iran, Iraq, Jordan, Oman, Yemen, Kuwait,

Lebanon, Mauritania, Morocco, Saudi Arabia, Somalia, Sudan and Syria mobilised and activated social networks to protest with varying degrees of vehemence. Egypt's Mubarak was toppled. These were ordinary people, organising in large numbers, defying the armies, sinister militia forces and police thugs that once terrorised them. In Cairo's Tahrir (Liberation) Square and other zones of other cities, they shaped public spaces, a world they could only once dream of. There was a large presence of women among the demonstrators, women who had been consigned to the domestic sphere in which they bore the humiliation of their men and gave birth to sons and daughters of poverty. These were women with a new feeling of empowerment.

This "volcano of rage" – a term coming from the 1960s Pan-Arabist anthem – was not just a particular expression of Arab or Islamic outrage, or a phenomenon guided by religious or political leaders but a claim for something that is the officially declared right of all people: to live in dignity. These are countries whose youthful populations, like those of the rest in the world, face unpromising and even frightening futures. Betrayed by the ruling elites, they have been, as the late Syrian playwright Saadallah Wannous once said, "sentenced to hope". But hope and despair come cheap, as the old saying goes, and when entrenched elites start toying with the people's hopes the lie is soon laid bare. In March 2009, Muammar Gaddafi hosted a summit meeting of Arab heads of state. The final declaration – evidently drafted with "diplomatic" ends – called for adopting a proposal by the Tunisian president to declare 2010 the "Year of Youth" and the leaders stressed the need to "establish the culture of openness and the acceptance of the other, and to support the principles of fraternity, tolerance and respect of human values that emphasize human rights, respect human dignity, and protect human freedom".[5] The barefaced cynicism of these words soon helped to kill any hope that may have survived till then and began to fuel the despair and anger that would take the form of the "volcano of rage". Mohamed Bouazizi's anguish, his sister explained, came from long experience of being "humiliated and insulted and not allowed to live". The spectre that is now haunting the world and in particular the tyrants who are falling, or who fear falling, who scramble to save their billions in overseas accounts and to find a palace in which to live under the protection of another tyrant, is the spectre of the down-trodden, the reviled, of those who have not been "allowed to live", and who are now starting to organise and to call for the most basic of rights: the right to a dignified existence.

To echo the other Manifesto once again – not least because history repeats itself since we are not a species that is particularly willing to learn from its self-made disasters – two things result from the appearance of this spectre:

I.   The right to human dignity is now being acknowledged as being itself a power;

II.   It is high time for human rights to take on their radical essence, to show openly "in the face of the whole world" their claims and strengths, to "meet the nursery tale" they have so far been, to fight back against the swindle they have become with everyday warping of their terms and routine abuse with a clarion call asserting their real nature. If "the history of all hitherto existing society is the history of class struggle", it is also the history of human rights abuse. History has given humanity a series of declarations and covenants recognising different kinds of human rights. However, they are usually denatured by being divided up into generations or families, and bestowed from above as something floating around outside social, and especially juridical, institutions as if they are merely a concession from our leaders, from the privileged.

No, human rights are not divisible because they all stem from one basic right, applicable to every human being: the right to a dignified existence. No, they are not a gift, not charity in their present traduced form of humanitarianism, but a basic human requirement. No, they are not outside social institutions but must be their basis, and the basis of any democratic republic is the freedom of all its citizens in the true and human sense of the word. Deprived of the means of a dignified existence, no human being can be free. Rights are the basis of dignity, freedom and justice on nothing less than a universal scale. Rights are radical.

I

The People Versus Neoliberalism

Neoliberalism is, of course, not the only politico-economic system in the history of the world that has inflicted grave, systematic human rights violations. Concentrated political and economic power is, by definition, inimical to universal human rights. Hence, Soviet and Chinese Communism, too, engineered human rights violations on a massive scale. Among the crimes of Stalin's regime were its general terror tactics; the purge of the Great Terror from 1936 – 1939 in which KGB figures show that nearly 700,000 people were executed; the forced labour camps through which millions of Soviet citizens passed and in which well over two million people are estimated to have died; the ethnic cleansing of the Second World War in which a million Chechens, Crimean Tatars, Balkars, Kalmiks, and Turks were deported from their homelands to Central Asia and about forty per cent died along the way; and the project of collectivisation in the name of "progress", the insane "socialist mode of production" – in which, as in neoliberalism, people didn't count – that ultimately led to the deaths and deportation of between five and eight million people and took an additional enormous toll in the famine years of 1932 and 1933 when it is calculated that some six to eight million peasants died in Ukraine and Central Asia.

In Mao Zedong's China (as in the Soviet Union) human rights were sacrificed to progress and "national" uniformity. The latter project led to the brutal repression of competing regional and ideological movements, including the invasion of Tibet in 1950. Mao's "development" plan, known as the Great Leap Forward (1958), was an attempt to emulate Stalin's collectivisation. Between 1958 and 1960 millions of people died as the result of famine and several million of these deaths are attributed to the regime Mao inflicted on the rural population. As Mao's personality cult hardened into the Cultural Revolution (1966), there were countless more victims. Estimates of deaths caused by Mao-style communism between 1950 and 1976 range from forty to seventy million and to that horrific toll must be added all the suffering caused by different kinds of persecution, including prisons and "re-education" camps.

Decades of contempt for human rights in bringing about this kind of "progress" would have greatly facilitated Deng Xiaoping's remarkable turnaround in the 1990s when, in pushing for his own brand of regime, also in the name of "progress", he claimed that China's biggest threat was from the "left". Pushing his pro-"reform" slogan "Let some people get rich first", he soon had the country reeling from one anti-human rights, "stability maintenance" system to another in which the beneficiaries are few and the victims legion. In Russia's case, without any prior culture of human rights, the post-1989 Kremlin has become a money-making machine in which organised crime is one of the mainstays of a patently wonky latter-day tsardom (or stardom perhaps) headed by a wannabe James Bond who bares his chest for carefully staged alpha-male photo ops featuring horses, tigers, bears and whales. Yet many observers inside Russia noted that the Kremlin was greatly alarmed by the Arab Spring, a judgement which would seem to be borne out by the imprisonment of three members of the not very tigerish punk-rock collective Pussy Riot whom Putin deems to have undermined the country's moral foundations. One real indicator of the moral foundations of these two countries is the extraordinary imprecision of the estimates, involving tens of millions of victims of their "progress", which not only suggests cover-ups of systematic massive violations of human rights but also that, when it comes to the needs of the regime – communist, reformist, kleptocratic or whatever form it takes – which is to say the needs of those who hold power, the victims have no human value.

Human rights violations everywhere are an expression of power relations on the individual, community, national and global scales, taking many forms from the master-slave relationship, domestic violence, abuse of children, pogroms, xenophobic attacks, through to killing people on the other side of the globe in drone attacks. They are committed by rough hands dripping blood and soft, "clean", well-manicured hands that pick up telephones and press buttons. The chief shared ingredient in all the different types of abuse is denial or a downgrading of the victim's human dignity in a mental construction and/or by means of many kinds of physical ill-treatment that annihilate or diminish the victim. Racist and sexist violence are just two examples of this. The neoliberal system commits human rights crimes on an inconceivable scale because its reach extends throughout the planet. Indeed, as argued below, it routinely commits every officially listed crime against humanity and covers them up where possible. Besides the evident state and big-business routine control of the media, official responses – and, in particular, that of the United States – to Wikileaks and other whistleblowers, are instances of present-day attempts to cover up human rights crimes, for example the practice known by the horrible euphemism "extraordinary rendition", namely the abduction and illegal transfer of a person from one nation to another to be submitted to secret offshore torture. The focus, here, is on the neoliberal system because that is what we have now and because it is also the first truly global system of economic and political control. Nobody can escape its clutches.

The Rome Statute of the International Criminal Court (1998),[6] Article 7 ("Crimes against Humanity"), Part 2 ("Jurisdiction, Admissibility and Applicable Law"), states:

A "'crime against humanity' means any of the following acts when committed as part of a widespread or systematic attack directed against any civilian population, with knowledge of the attack:

(a) Murder;

(b) Extermination;

(c) Enslavement;

(d) Deportation or forcible transfer of population;

(e) Imprisonment or other severe deprivation of physical liberty in violation of fundamental rules of international law;

(f) Torture;

(g) Rape, sexual slavery, enforced prostitution, forced pregnancy, enforced sterilization, or any other form of sexual violence of comparable gravity;

(h) Persecution against any identifiable group or collectivity on political, racial, national, ethnic, cultural, religious, gender as defined in paragraph 3, or other grounds that are universally recognized as impermissible under international law, in connection with any act referred to in this paragraph or any crime within the jurisdiction of the Court;

(i) Enforced disappearance of persons;

(j) The crime of apartheid;

(k) Other inhumane acts of a similar character intentionally causing great suffering, or serious injury to body or to mental or physical health."

The Case against Neoliberalism

The increasingly untrammelled industrial society that sprang from feudalism has now spawned neoliberalism on a global scale, a system in which the supreme freedom is granted to an abstract non-human – anti-human – entity called The Market. In a regime in which human rights were respected and practised, markets (real markets are plural, not monolithic) could be an instrument of exchange which, like any other social or political institution, would be regulated so as not to permit abuse of the human subjects participating therein. In the unregulated neoliberal system, human beings are objects to be exploited like any other product. This market-being, as opposed to the human being, is well portrayed by Ernst Bloch's description of the man who has attained completely free will: a man "for whom external circumstances did not even have the force of accessory causes, such a nondetermined man would not be a free man but a fool and a public danger. He would be one completely irresponsible and full of incalculable blabberings; he would not be a creator but rather the inverse – he would be the image and model of chaos."[7] Anything can happen in The Market, the instrument of such a man, and if some people in this faceless, secretive system are ever held accountable for its failures, disasters and destruction, they are usually minor figures used as scapegoats. The Market is never blamed, at least not by its masters. The neoliberal system is a rogue system, like the rogue elephant, an aberrant animal with violent, destructive tendencies that shuns its own group and rampages out of control. Neoliberalism has spurned human values and embraced one non-human one: money. What profit can be made out of using a human being, or "warehousing" a human being, or eliminating a human being? It is, therefore, inimical to human rights.

This view of people as instruments or obstacles takes on a brutal physical presence in all the mechanisms of exclusion, the walls and the border patrols. Day after day, aspiring immigrants or refugees, dispossessed sons and daughters of now-ravaged former colonial cornucopias of the western powers, are turned back, criminalised, dumped in the desert, drowned as they try to cross seas in frail boats, or exploited by human traffickers in their quest for a decent way of life. Libya's Muammar Gaddafi, for example, had tacit agreements with the European "democracies" to "warehouse" African immigrants (thus committing crimes against humanity according to the Rome Statute – henceforth RS

– Article 7, Part 2, d, e, h, i, j, k) whom he then threatened to free, as if they were counters in a game. The system has ripped apart the core Enlightenment values that have informed the notion of human rights for centuries. We are faced with a choice: neoliberalism or universal human rights. We can't have both.

Human rights don't exist in a "soft power" bubble as something to be doled out only when co-opting or hoodwinking people looks like a better deal than coercing them. Since the 2011 democratic uprisings in the Arab countries new and old oppressive rulers, when not resorting to outright repression as usual, have been trying to tamp down the revolts by bargaining with selected human rights, for example releasing political prisoners, lowering food prices and promising democratic reforms. Yet human rights can be hard power, if only enough people knew it. Their deep roots in the politics and economics of national and international systems have been revealed. They are being demanded across national borders and the national powers are trying to contain them. This situation spotlights the conflicts that have arisen between universal human rights and traditional conceptions of national sovereignty since the nation-state has ceased to be the only or main guarantor of human rights within its bounds. Just one more aspect of today's globalised system, this mismatch might be placed on the positive side of the balance since, as a transnational claim, the call for real human rights is much more than a matter of domestic politics and, to this extent, difficult to manage for old systems of state repression and, unlike other international initiatives, it is not coming from the top or for reasons of Realpolitik, but from a powerful, growing groundswell of ordinary, indignant citizens.

In general, the official practice of internationalised human rights today is in great part subsumed to the "humanitarian intervention" which is, of course, inextricable from national policy and economic interests. Things are changing now, and at the base of society. Only a fool would try to deny that many people of North Africa and the Middle East are united in claiming human rights, freedom, democracy and liberation from oppression. In the media, the missing piece of the story, as the West purports to support their struggles, is that it was the western "democracies" that coddled their tyrants as long as the profits were high. In the case of Libya after much delay, and pressure from President Nicholas Sarkozy – who needed some face-saving polish after he had offered to send anti-riot police to help crush the earlier uprising in Tunisia (RS: a, e, k) – the United Nations Resolution 1973 imposed a no-fly zone, an arms embargo, an assets freeze and other sanctions while "all necessary measures" were supposedly taken to protect its citizens. It is not as if Gaddafi's violent kleptocracy has been a secret for the last four decades. Then again, if Faure Gnassingbe, President of Togo (elected in not very democratic circumstances) was going from alley to alley, house to house to punish rebels "without pity", as Gaddafi swore to do in Libya, there would be no talk, let alone imposition, of no-fly zones. Togo, as far as we know, doesn't have oil.

Humanitarianism is not human rights but in many ways their opposite. Humanitarianism is a postmodern form of nineteenth-century charity, selectively offered or imposed from outside on a temporary basis. Human rights, in contrast, are proclaimed as intrinsic to the human being, and therefore inalienable and inviolable. If they are to be claimed as such, they must also be understood as such and saved from the barefaced hypocrisy, if not contempt with which they tend to be treated, and given back their rightful good name.

The neoliberal system is, by its very nature, hostile to human rights. The cock-and-bull story that human rights exist in this system only gives them a bad name. They, like people, are in thrall to an unjust system that subjects them to its tyranny and cynically condemns them to a marginal existence. If human rights as they are permitted to exist today were given human form, they might look like the men found in the Omarska iron mine in northern Bosnia (RS: a, c, e, h, i, k) in the summer of 1992, almost fifty years after the appalling images of the inmates of Nazi concentration camps that led to the cry "Never again!" and, eventually, to the Universal Declaration of Human Rights. The Muslim captives in the Serbian camp of Omarska, to whom the journalists cannot give the name "men" but, rather, refer to them as "beings" or "fantastic, rediscovered beasts", are rotting alive, joints protruding through festering skin, their blazing, accusing gaze being the only way they can tell the terrible truth of what has been done to them. Referring to the Auschwitz inmate, Primo Levi asked, "Is this a man?" The answer must be "Yes". One Omarska prisoner, approached by a journalist and watched by brawny machine-gun-bearing guards, waved him away saying, "I do not want to tell lies and I cannot tell the truth".[8] The man was declaring his dignity. The "rediscovered beasts" are the armed goon-guards who – in denying the dignity of other *human* "beings", have renounced any dignity that might be called "human". Truth is also being battered out of human rights as they are forged on an infernal anvil into yet another instrument of neoliberalism. Yet they, too, have their blazing, accusing dignity.

Neoliberalism, today's system of widely deregulated free-market capitalism, makes a commodity of everything from which profit might be wrung, including human beings (RS: a, b, c, d, e, f, g, h, i, j, k) who are envisaged as mere instruments to be exploited to this end. This automatically eliminates the founding principles of human rights, freedom and dignity, because the system's fast-accumulating vast fortunes are founded on fast-spreading desperate impoverishment (RS: a, c (sometimes), d (sometimes), g (sometimes), h (sometimes), j (sometimes), k). Its institutions are mostly limited to protecting, by force if necessary, armour-clad and secretive property rights of the haves who have stripped the have-nots of theirs (RS: k, at least). Yet literature and sometimes history tell us, even if the economists do not, that great fortunes tend to be based on old (and new) crimes, military adventures, slavery, spoliation of the public domain, lying cheating, betrayal and all the ugliest of human proclivities, activities and attributes.

Neoliberalism is, in a nutshell, bad "economics" a word that was originally related with good household management. It has no foresight. It has contempt for notions of producing and conserving, and adamantly shuns that of sharing, the essence of social life. The human household is a mess: many of its members are dying of dispossession and neglect and its garden is ravaged by every imaginable kind of wanton ransacking, as if losing glaciers, rivers, jungles and plant and animal species had no consequences, as if no one had ever heard Prospero's warning: "the great globe itself, / Yea, all which it inherit, shall dissolve".[9] Neoliberal accumulation doesn't come about through productive activities as they were once understood but through plunder (RS: h, k, at least) and the intangible insanity of finance speculation. In many societies, food traditionally means the social activities of production, preparation and sharing. Now, speculation in abstract food commodities has pushed prices up to the highest they've been in thirty years. Pension funds, hedge funds and investment banks like Goldman Sachs and Morgan Stanley dominate food markets, and the sums of money involved vastly exceed the amount traded by real food producers and buyers, to the tune of twenty times the total figure disbursed by all countries for agricultural "aid". In 2009, Goldman Sachs earned £340 million from food speculation.[10]

This is a clean-hands crime against humanity. As the Spanish writer Juan José Millás sums it up, investment banks can push up or smash down the value of your crop two years before you have even planted it, can buy a non-existent crop from you, without your even knowing, and sell it to a string of others and you don't get a cent out of it, though you'll go to prison, hang or commit suicide for them if they decide to sink you. You are a commodity and, "Once you become an object it matters little whether you have children or parents, whether you woke up with a touch or fever, whether you're in the middle of a divorce, or haven't slept because you're studying for some examination to qualify for a job. None of this counts for the finance economy or the economic terrorist who has just put his finger on the map or on a country – who cares where – and says 'I'll buy' or 'I'm selling', with all the impunity of a Monopoly player, acquiring or shedding fake real estate …"[11]

In this system human rights are given with declarations and snatched away by the real world. As great fortunes are made, human rights are trashed. Still worse, there is a racist skewing of the abuse, as a quick glance at the list of the world's twenty poorest countries shows (RS: a, b, c, d, e, h, j, k and sometimes g). Most of the victims are dark-skinned but are usually subsumed as a colour-free group called "the poor" because such real-world, massive-scale racism doesn't fit with the glowing myth of universality of rights.

Re-appropriating human rights and respect for human dignity, if enforced, would of necessity put an end to crimes committed in the name of "progress" but which, in reality, take us back to a state of pre-Enlightenment barbarity. The crime novelist Don Winslow sums up the situation in words that career economists seem unable to use:

[…] there are two worlds:
The savage
The less savage.
The savage is the world of pure power, survival of the fittest, drug cartels and death squads, dictators and strongmen, terrorist attacks, gang wars, tribal hatred, mass murder, mass rape.
The less savage is the world of pure civilized power, govern-

ments and armies, multinationals and banks, oil companies, shock-and-awe, death-from-the-sky, genocide, mass economic rape.
[...]
They're the same world.[12]

If neoliberalism doesn't permit human rights to flourish, let us all claim universal rights so that neoliberalism can't flourish.

Kings, Coltan, Killing Fields "and all that stuff": Neoliberalism Past and Present

The grotesque forms taken by neoliberalism today didn't drop out of a clear blue sky but have deep, dark, tangled roots in abuses of the past that were committed with impunity, or one might say "freely" in the present-day travesty of the word "freedom". As a result, the crimes kept mounting. One of the world's poorest countries today is just one example among countless others that shows, in the tragic sense, how closely human rights are bound with political economy and, accordingly, how they can only be recovered by political action. King Leopold II of Belgium (1835 – 1909) arrayed himself with the adjective "humanitarian" as he set about his "civilising mission" in his private fiefdom of the "Belgian" Congo which he never visited. In reality, he was the crimes-against-humanity king who paid mercenaries to enslave the Congolese people by means of wholesale murder, terror, rape and mutilation (RS: a, b, c, d, e, f, g, h, i, j, k). By the time he relinquished his private ownership of the colony to the State of Belgium in 1908, an estimated ten million people had died in the making of his vast personal fortune, which was obtained mainly by direct exploitation of mines and rubber plantations and the indirect leasing of conces-sions to private companies that paid him fifty per cent of their profits.

In his independence speech in 1960, the new Prime Minister

Patrice Lumumba shocked the Belgian delegation by denouncing the hideous crimes committed in Africa by the "humanitarian king" and his European accomplices. He was telling the truth but the truth wasn't welcome. He also revoked the 25,000-member exclusively Belgian Officer Corps as being inimical to the interests of an independent nation. This truth wasn't welcome either. He told the truth and died for it. Lumumba was captured, tortured and murdered and his body was never recovered.[13]

In the waning days of the Eisenhower Administration, Washington's man Mobutu Sese Seko, the former colonial police informer and future five-times-over billionaire and "embodiment of the nation" in a leopard skin cap, temporarily seized power in 1960, and eventually completed his coup in 1965 with the help of mercenaries financed by the United States and covert assistance from the CIA. The Congo became Zaire and its absolute ruler Mobutu a poster child forerunner of the noxious spirit of neoliberalism and inspiration of the term "kleptocracy" because of his looting of the state treasury and national industries as he sold off the country's immense mineral wealth including copper, cobalt, diamonds, as well as 64% of the world's supplies of columbite-tantalite (coltan), which is essential in the manufacture of mobile phones and other electronic devices, not to mention his bids for grandiose and eventually pie-in-the-sky public works, such as the Inga Dam, which was supposed to produce a third of the world's hydroelectric power.

As the country fell further into debt, Mobutu simply re-, re- and reshuffled his cabinet and printed new currency, while the capitalist powers kept him supplied with arms to put down rebellions. In May 1990, he ordered his death squads to massacre dozens of protesting students from the campus of Lubumbashi University in the copper-rich, secessionist-tending province of Katanga (now Shaba – RS: a, k). Yet, Mobutu, praised by US President Reagan as a "voice of good sense and good will", was feted by every president from Eisenhower to George H. W. Bush, in part because he used the strategic position of his country, which is surrounded by nine other African nations, to contain Soviet influence in Africa by offering a haven for anti-communist guerrilla movements, particularly against oil-rich Angola. He was only abandoned by his powerful friends when the end of the Cold War rendered him no longer useful, after which he hired a Washington public relations firm to clean up his image. In the neoliberal system you can buy anything.

Mobutu, with the help of his western partners, bankrupted a very rich country for his personal benefit and was able to do so because he was armed, supported and covered for by the capitalist powers. Now, if he is remembered at all, he tends to be portrayed not as a partner of men in suits and ties in faraway air-conditioned offices but in a racist way, as a kind of monster-clown, a preposterous, vainglorious figure, who collected mansions around the world, invited large numbers of hangers-on to shopping trips in Paris or to cavort in Disneyland, and who built himself a white marble palace known as the "Versailles of the jungle" in his hometown of Gbadolite. His crimes against humanity are not spoken of because the heart of darkness that pumps out Congo's lifeblood beats in western banks, stock exchanges and multinational corporations.

Two men, King Leopold II and Mobutu, aided and abetted by "democratic" nations, brought the enormous rich land of Zaire, now Democratic Republic of the Congo, to its knees. Rich in natural resources, once the second-most industrialised country in Africa, it now has the lowest GDP per capita in the world ($348 in 2011) and was the theatre of "Africa's World War" (1998 – 2003), which involved seven foreign armies and, by 2008, had killed another 5.4 million people, mainly from disease and starvation, while millions more were displaced from their homes (RS: b, d, h, i, k). Today, in the globalisation of economic interests and war, exploitation of coltan, without which there would be no IT industry, far from bringing prosperity to the Congolese people, fuels the arms industry, has filled the coffers of the Rwandan Patriotic Army and vastly enriched some Ugandan military commanders and businessmen. Foreign multinational corporations buy the coltan from the rebels who use slaves to mine it (RS: c, d, e, k) and westerners provide weapons (RS: a, c, d, e, k) to maintain their illegal networks. This is not so much an "African" failure story as a neoliberal "success" story.

The chapter headings of the United Nations *Report on the Illegal Exploitation of Natural Resources and Other forms of Wealth of the Congo* (2001)[14] might be read as a mini-treatise on neoliberal functioning. They include "Pre-existing structures that facilitated illegal exploitation"; "Mass-scale looting"; "Systematic and systemic exploitation"; "Current structures of illegal exploitation"; "Individual actors"; "Economic data: confirmation of the illegal exploitation of the natural resources of the Democratic Republic of the Congo"; "Links between the exploitation of natural resources and the continuation of the conflict"; "Budgets compared to military expenditures"; "Financing the war"; "Special features of the links between the exploitation of natural resources and the continuation of the conflict"; and the slightly guilty-sounding "Facilitators or passive accomplices". There is no chapter specifically dealing with the country's history of human rights violations, or showing how the country as a whole has been and is submitted to impoverishment and war, or on the conditions of slavery in which the mines are worked by adults and children, or about the role of the western powers in all that.

The United Nations abstains from denouncing the neoliberal economic system and its multinational companies for the war crimes being committed in the Congo but goes so far as to describe them as "the engine of the conflict" (RS: b, d, k, at least). These enterprises include Cabor Corporation, OM Group, AVX, Eagle Wings Resources International, Trinitech International, Kemet Electronics Corporation, Viashay Sprague, all based in the

United States and they compete, *inter alia*, with Germany's HC Starc and EPCOS, China's Ningxia, and Traxys and George Forrest International of Belgium. They sell the processed coltan to such "reputable" companies as Nokia, Motorola, Compaq, Dell, Hewlett Packard, IBM, Lucent, Ericsson and Sony which produce computer chips, cell phones and game consoles. The blood is not only on the hands of the rogue militia leaders in Africa. It passes all the way along the line to consumers, automatically making an accomplice, usually unwitting, of everybody who owns these goods and who is increasingly dependent on them. Almost every consumer good in the neoliberal world is tainted with human rights abuse at some point in its production. Only the victims are free of the crime. In Baghdad, parents of children killed in bombing attacks scream, "What is the crime of our children who died?" The question is about injustice and it reverberates beyond the walls of these homes in which innocents die or are permanently maimed: what is wrong with the whole world?

One more example, a supposed success story of the neoliberal numbers smokescreen, Cambodia, shows once again what is so wrong with the world. This country lives in modern memory as the land of the Khmer Rouge "killing fields", as if the Khmer Rouge was a strictly local aberration. What is usually skipped over is the fact that Cambodia was subjected to tremendous carpet-bombing attacks between October 1965 and August 1973, in which some 2,756,941 tons of ordnance were dropped on 113,716 sites, of which at least ten per cent were indiscriminately targeted (RS: b). The country is still seeded with unexploded ordnance, which maims and kills farmers and renders valuable land useless (RS: k). Among the blowback effects was the rise of the Pol Pot regime and the "killing fields". It was subsequently the scene of a massive humanitarian operation overseen by the "international community". Now, with an economic growth rate averaging about 7% per year since the mid-1990s, it tends to be awarded the following neoliberal profile: despite the dubious human rights record (only sometimes mentioned) of the present government headed by the former Khmer Rouge member Hun Sen, Cambodia has opened up the most liberalised economy in Southeast Asia. It would be more accurate to say that *because* of human rights abuse the regime has managed to conjure up this so-called growth rate, but neoliberal language distorts everything and the question always begged is: growth of what for whom?

This is a regime denounced by Amnesty International for its torture of thousands of political prisoners (RS: e, f). It has orchestrated a land grab that has snatched away the livelihood of the rural poor (RS: d, h, k) so that, in this "growth" economy, at least thirty percent – some five million people – of Cambodia's population live well below the poverty line and many more only just above it. Naturally transparency and accountability do not feature in the process of land grabbing in this densely-populated country. However, it is clear that its extent is enormous. NGOs calculate that approximately half the arable land or more than two million hectares have been handed over to some 150 private companies, sometimes fronts for foreigners.[15] The title claims of small farmers are, of course, not part of the deal. Most of the country's rural population barely subsists on minute plots of land and foraging. Moreover, history has long shown that, because of traditional forms of the division of labour, when land is seized, poverty takes a female face.

What is on sale to foreigners in the very liberal economy of Cambodia? Government assets seized by the elite for its own benefit, for example universities, hospitals, ministry buildings, police stations, concessions for managing the ancient complex of Angor Wat and the Cheung Ek killing field, land, land and more land, forests, fishing grounds, reefs, islands, beaches, lakes, mining concessions, toxic dumps, and people, in a flourishing business in women, girls, boys and babies (RS: g). Villagers are summarily evicted from their land by bulldozers, their houses set alight and they are beaten if they protest. The country is a big-money Shangri-La for speculators turning their backs on paralysed western financial markets and transferring liquid assets to the East, seeking profits that soar above thirty per cent. Hedge funds, private equity funds, and property funds grow fat on tax holidays and an absence of money-laundering laws. Close to two thousand million dollars in foreign finance flowed into Cambodia in 2007. None of it went outside a very small circle of power. The effects were felt by millions because the investment was in dispossession (RS: d, h, k).

Approximately half of Cambodia's national budget comes from foreign governments and agencies whose well-paid members are concentrated in the capital Phnom Penh. Their lifestyle has created an artificial boom in the city, which translates into yet another burden to be borne by the rural population. Unlike Mobutu, Hun Sen has not needed to hire a public relations firm to maintain the studiedly benign face of his neoliberalism. Of course he can't resist the usual "great-leader" blandishments so his online biography informs the reader that he is a "a distinguished leader, loved by his people, who ... brings about national peace, stability, unity, economics and development in all sectors; defends democracy and achieves positive international cooperation; maintains and defends national independence, territorial integrity in accordance with the prospect of Sangkum Reast Niyum; ... and defending justice for the sustainability of the monarchy in the Kingdom of Cambodia,"[16] whatever "justice" "for the sustainability of the monarchy" might mean. In any case, lying is one of his lesser crimes. Not that his international supporters are concerned about that. His repression has created a "secure" environment for tourists who can pay his lessees to see Angkor Wat and the killing fields while his cordial relations with the rulers of Japan, China, the United States, Russia, France and Australia, et cetera – the so-called "international community" – along with the aid they shower on him supposedly give a rosy glow of legitimacy to the great business opportunities he offers.

Cambodia hasn't left barbarism behind. In terms of basic human rights, the abuses of the past, now with a new name and new players, are casting a long shadow over the future of millions of its people. They are not just home-grown but also perpetrated by the jackals of neoliberalism like the British currency broker who saw there was a fortune to be made from suffering: "I loved the deal from the start. Let's be honest, who wants 6%? I wanted a deal that would wake me up in the night, sweating. We could make good money [...] There was a buzz about Cambodia you don't get elsewhere. It's Cambodia, the killing fields and all that stuff. Something different to show your mates back home. I show them the visa in my passport. I have something they don't."[17] Killing fields "and all that stuff" are a "buzz". This is the language of neoliberalism.

The Democratic Republic of the Congo and Cambodia are just two cases in a generalised process that has reached into all corners of the world. Everything that was once *common* to real human *commun*ities, including land, water, forests, minerals, indigenous knowledge and the structure of life itself in genetic resources, along with public services such as health care, education, transport, and water and sewerage services, is privatised. Human beings are commodities and can be put on to the markets of human trafficking, sex slavery, child labour, surrogate motherhood, baby and child trafficking, and human organ sales (RS: a, b, c, d, e, f, g, h, i, j, k). Or they simply stand in the way of profit-making.

Who has heard of the genocide (RS: a, b, d, e, f, g, h, i, j, k) that has been occurring for almost fifty years in West Papua, where the indigenous people are an awkward obstacle to neoliberal "progress", which is euphemistically called "mining industry" or "forestry industry"? A 2004 report by the Yale Law School, *Indonesian Human Rights Abuses in West Papua: Application of the Law of Genocide to the History of Indonesian Control*,[18] concludes that "the historical and contemporary evidence [...] strongly suggests that the Indonesian government has committed proscribed acts with the intent to destroy the West Papuans as such, in violation of the 1948 Convention on the Prevention and Punishment of the Crime of Genocide and the customary international law prohibition this Convention embodies." Genocide? How come we don't know about it? Doesn't it matter? Is there really such a thing as human rights? Genocide committed with impunity would seem to suggest that the answer is "no". The not-so-secret "industry" in West Papua is murder, torture and plunder and, along the global chain, it is sustained by the international arms industry that enables the Indonesian regime to continue on its murderous course. The genocide may not be well known (shame on the media!) but there have always been some voices clamouring against the crimes being committed in this beautiful country, yet their protests have usually fallen on deaf or indifferent ears. Why? Don't we have human rights declarations and an International Criminal Court? Haven't we advanced beyond pre-Enlightenment thought? Are we still mired in the thinking of people like Saint Augustine (354 – 430) for whom, "The prime cause, then, of slavery is sin, which brings man under the dominion of his fellow" (RS: c, retroactively) because it was a consequence of the Fall of Man?[19] Does the supposed Original Sin of two historically dubious forebears exclude the West Papuans from the rights proclaimed in the "Universal" Declaration? Slavery is not caused by but *is* the "fall of man". The harsh reality is that human rights are only for some and if those of us who do enjoy them don't recognise the duty of calling for and protecting the rights of others, the circle of the lucky ones will keep shrinking more and more and the greedy ones will keep grabbing more and more. And where will humanity be then?

Commodities can be intangible and secret, increasingly taking the form of financial transactions, speculation with individual and sovereign debt and such ethereal items as futures and options. State functions become police functions in protecting private assets. Central bankers and other policy directors give priority to the financial sector above all else, opposing any plan that might reduce the value of their assets and their income, which is based on interest. As those assets and income burgeon, workers are obliged to accept lower and lower wages under pressure of fast-rising unemployment levels (RS: k). In a just world, the people who have brought about this situation would be the ones losing their jobs.

Human rights are not universal but the neoliberal market system is. This is a global tissue of economic interdependencies, essentially above and beyond *human* control, a phantas-magorical, supposedly impartial entity that governs everything. Today's "actors" aren't autonomous human beings going about their own life plans but financial actors in many guises, such as corporations, multinational business alliances, invisible entities, rogue traders and financial consortia shaping economic policies that affect every person on planet without any possibility, let alone right, of questioning them.

With origins going back to the aftermath of the First World War when mortgage lending, buttressed by Cold War anti-worker ideology, began to move in on the economic territory of industry and commerce, today's neo-rentier economy could also be described as a neo-feudal form of debt serfdom, in both economic terms and in the pre-Enlightenment values it espouses. Even the name "neoliberal" is misleading because early econo-mists who are sometimes described as "liberal", John Stuart Mill, for example, were actually concerned with regulation, keeping a proper balance between prices and costs, and protecting the markets from rentier and unbridled capitalist interests.

A baleful phenomenon called "finance" has snatched control of the economic sphere, of industry, real estate and government, and has come to be seen as an autonomous force making money all by itself. This involves stealth, absence of accountability and ideological conquest, mainly centring on a distorted, deranged idea of "freedom" in which freedom to speculate on the market means freeing the market of any obstacles that might get in the way of trade and profit, human rights for example. Financial wealth, which is actually debt in terms of a society's means of production and income, is presented as a tangible, productive part of the real economy, when it is little more than figures feverishly ticking over on stock exchange screens – 5,000 transactions in the time it takes to blink.[20] For the banker, the ideal state is when the whole economy is capitalised, when economic surplus is paid out as interest (in particular to bankers) rather than being reinvested in productive activity.

The enormity of the risks of such speculation can be seen in the gambling that occurs, for example, in the New York Clearing House and Chicago Mercantile Exchange in which every day the equivalent of a whole year's GDP of the United States changes hands at lightning speed dictated by computer calculations. That the system is open to fraud is hardly surprising. In the case of the sub-prime mortgage loans in the United States, involving "respectable" banks and ratings agencies, the majority were found by the FBI (Federal Bureau of Investigation) to have given fraudulent ratings involving around $US750 billion in the financial meltdown of 2008 – 2009.[21] The perpetrating financial institutions, far from being punished, were given a $US13 trillion bailout which was presented as if it were essential to sustaining the industrial economy. Mohamed Bouazizi was a better economist. He understood something the classical political economists taught, which is that the productive base of a society isn't created by a bunch of compulsive gamblers posing as bank executives but requires workers with jobs, and that the real causes of economic disaster should be sought in undue concentrations of wealth, property and income, earned and unearned. In the neoliberal system, criminal financiers get huge golden handshakes and the already castigated workers are further scapegoated and penalised. All this is inextricably bound with human rights and the problem lies at the rotten core of the neoliberal capitalist economy.

As the figures of financial transactions flit through cyberspace, it may seem at first glance that they have little to do with ordinary mortals. Eastern Europe and the former Soviet Union, however, offer an example of how the power of faraway finance affects people's real living conditions. When the IMF imposed its "shock therapy" after 1989, thrusting on to totally unprepared ground its imposition of The Market, the number of people living in poverty in these countries trebled to a figure of a hundred million. This policy aided and abetted a form of mafia capitalism in Russia and Central Asia along with deeply entrenched, corrupt regimes in a mutated guise of authoritarianism, affecting some eighty per cent of the peoples of the former Soviet Union.[22] The backwards slide in democracy indicators includes severe censorship, rigged elections and government-controlled courts, while political dissent is systematically suppressed.

Inextricably bound with the real economy, the "nursery tale" of human rights is a real-life horror story where a sociopathic serial killer, the finance economy, strangles human rights with the garrotte of murderous speculation and parasitism as it mercilessly slashes public spending to death, asserting that it is "unproductive" when, in fact, transport, health and educational systems are the lifeblood of a truly productive economy. It injects its poison into the education system (for example, by discouraging critical thinking, excluding the history of economic thought from the university curriculum and constantly pushing its own sinister fairytale of the rugged individualist, rags-to-riches, self-made man) and, of course, the press.

To give one example of despotic control over the press, without needing to cite the usual suspects, Fox News or Rupert Murdoch, Australia's richest person, a mining magnate called

Gina Rinehart (with a fortune of $US 2.4 billion and growing fast) has bought stakes in Fairfax and Ten Media in order to become a public commentator on what is good for "the nation". This means that she can rail against taxes on super-profits and profess her view that Australia needs "guest labour". What she has in mind is something akin to indentured labour (RS: c, e, j, k) which, she believes, should be semi-skilled and confined to hot and remote areas in a "Northern Economic Zone". This reserve would effectively function as a state of exception, more or less isolated from the world, in which the combination of semi-slave labour and subsistence wages would save "the nation" from rising prices. She recently called on Australian workers to accept lower wages because "African workers are willing to earn just $2 a day".[23] Gina Rinehart, like her fellow rich people, also thinks that the very wealthy should receive special tax benefits because they are the motor of the economy as income "earners". The parasites, they say, are the "lazy" welfare recipients who should be discouraged by having their benefits removed because they represent "unproductive" state spending: no rights for the poor because they don't deserve them.

In the twenty-first century, states are institutionally weak, dominated by "the market" and characterised by economic crime and corruption. They, too, often function as states of exception in which legal systems are ignored and there are no holds barred. This breeds violence that their feeble public institutions are not equipped to confront, so "security" (of the rich) is increasingly enforced by private enterprise along with state military and paramilitary bodies. In South Africa, by 1999, there were four security guards for every uniformed police member. Here, in the country with one of the "best and fairest" constitutions in the world, the private army represented by the security sector has more people under arms than the armed forces, with rich whites among the best-paying clients, so the divide is along racial lines. Social systems are violently torn apart into the division between the few haves and the many have-nots, and further fragmented by all the conflicts that arise between people who are forced to scrabble to make a living in a dehumanised world (RS: k).

In terms of numbers alone the results are dreadful enough. Yet we need to be more shocked. If one is to be truly human, one must perform a feat of imagination and recall that every number we use when we are trying to describe the plight of the dispossessed represents people with names, faces, families, stories and feelings, people like us, anybody, a real-life Mohamed Bouazizi, who is "not allowed to live". Every single digit making up the statistics of tragedy – poverty, homelessness, hunger, deaths, the tortured, the maimed by mines, the displaced, the refugees, the enslaved, and all the forms of abuse visited on human beings by their fellows – each digit, inextricably bound with the flicking numbers in stock exchanges, represents the suffering of a unique, a special human being and its injurious effects on all the people in relation with that person. Suffering is not an amorphous mass but is thrust into individual human flesh-and-blood containers, each one designated by a name, a singular genetic structure, a personality, a particular way of walking, smiling, looking and loving, one plus one plus one plus one plus one ... until they become billions of humans in distress. Subtract a few thousand and it makes no difference to the pain of those who are left because their affliction is unique to each one of them. This is why human rights and dignity have to be universal. Otherwise justice has absconded.

If human rights are to foster the "spirit of brotherhood" of the Universal Declaration of Human Rights, empathy is needed, the ability to put ourselves into other skins and feel what it would be like to eke out a bare existence without knowing where the next bite to eat is coming from, to be dependent on the caprices of or subjected to the cruelty of others, to slave your life away in horrendous conditions, to watch your children wasting or dying of hunger, diarrhoea, malaria and other easily preventable diseases. Mohamed Bouazizi's denunciation of the system shocked many people because self-immolation is an appalling act of despair. Also appalling are selling children into slavery and prostitution, forced labour (RS: c, e, g, h, k) and all the other atrocities of neoliberalism. Is our imagination so limited that we are mute before these crimes, that we can't shout that this must not happen, that everybody has rights? Can't those who enjoy rights claim for the rightless and excluded, for anybody and for everybody, the rights that are supposed to be universal? Some idea of the figures involved is given below, but they are not just abstract ciphers. They speak of human beings. We need to try to conceive what it feels like to try to survive in the conditions the numbers only hint at. The exercise should be unbearable.

- In 2008, the World bank estimated[24] that over 3 billion people (almost 50% of the world's population) subsisted on $2.50 or less per day, a figure that would be much worse four years on;
- In 2007, the poorest 40 per cent of the world's population accounted for 5 percent of global income. The richest 20 per cent accounted for three-quarters of world income;[25]
- Nearly a billion people entered the 21st century unable to read a book or sign their names;[26]
- Over 30,000 children (this is "only" those *under the age of five*) die each day (nearly eleven million per year, equalling the child population of France, Germany, Greece and Italy combined) due to poverty (RS: a, b, k). "They die quietly in some of the poorest villages on earth, far removed from the scrutiny and the conscience of the world. Being meek and weak in life makes these dying multitudes even more invisible in death."[27]

Neoliberalism – economic liberalisation, free trade, open markets, deregulation, or whatever you want to call it – was always understood as "a position of disparity". Ten months before the Universal Declaration of Human Rights was proclaimed, George Kennan, architect of the Marshall Plan and head of the US State Department's Director of Policy Planning, saw what was coming, the mirage of an apparently unified world dominated by the great powers, first in the form of states and then corporations.

> We have about 50% of the world's wealth, but only 6.3% of its population.[...] Our real task in the coming period is to devise a pattern of relationships which will permit us to maintain this position of disparity.[...] We should cease to talk about vague and [...] unreal objectives such as human rights, the raising of the living standards, and democratization. The day is not far off when we are going to have to deal in straight power concepts. The less we are then hampered by idealistic slogans, the better."[28]

The Declaration of 1948 was stillborn for, even in gestation, it was condemned to languish among "unreal objectives", sacrificed to "straight power concepts" because disparity of wealth had to be maintained. "Idealistic slogans" and the "nursery tale" of human dignity for everybody therefore had to be consigned to the dump of dangerous dreams where the social architect Kennan believed they belonged.

The notion of the nation-state on which the human rights doctrine is founded has changed. We are witnessing not only the weakening of the nation-state but the concurrent strengthening of the transnational market and of financial actors who, through companies or multinational alliances, financial consortia, lobbying cabals like the shadowy Bilderberg Group, and even individual action, define the economic policies that influence the whole planet. The one-dimensional neoliberal credo is well consolidated and preparing to face new and uncertain scenarios within the framework of economic and political globalisation.

In feudal times, rulers reinforced by a bevy of Lords and Bishops claimed a "Divine Right" to deprive their subjects of their freedom, heavily taxing citizens and not permitting peasants to own the land on and from which they lived so that they were mired in poverty and dependency. It was only when they began to tax the wealthy to finance their power and rapacity that the elites were forced to see the political nature of the connection between their property and their freedoms. Today it's The Market that has the Divine Right that dispossesses people of their property, and the "Crisis" now gathers middle-class American (foreclosed) homeowners in its toxic embrace. It took a revolution to end feudalism and, in that revolution, the intimate connection between property and freedom was not lost: Maximilien Robespierre couldn't have been clearer. If it threatens freedom, property is not legitimate and, at the root of the destruction of freedom, is great economic inequality, "the source of all evils", he said.[29] In his speech on subsistence of 2 December 1792 he asks, "What is the primary aim of society? It is to maintain the inalienable rights of man. What is the foremost of these rights? The right to exist. Therefore the first social law is that which guarantees to all members of society the means of existence; all others are subordinate to that; property was instituted and guaranteed only in order to cement that law; if property is held it is first of all to live. And it is not true that property can ever be in opposition to the subsistence of men". Robespierre is usually presented today as the daddy of all devils, probably because his truth is glaring, irrefutable, especially if seen from the standpoint of universal human rights. Private property should never snatch the "subsistence of men". Would that not be the statement of a just man?

Today a handful of individuals can challenge national and international orders and move against the subsistence of citizens in order to impose their own interests. This is a major cause of extreme poverty, not to mention outright slavery (RS: c, d, g, h, k).[30] If human beings have any valid claims of need at all, they must be the elementary claims of the subsistence and basic security that permit freedom, the basic rights that Henry Shue defines as "... everyone's minimal, reasonable demands on others [...] the rational basis for justified demands the denial of which no self-respecting person can reasonably be expected to accept." If rights are reasonable, justified and a matter of self-respect, which is to say human dignity, then we all have the duty to ensure that every single human being enjoys the "rights to those things without which one cannot enjoy any other rights".[31]

The German philosopher Thomas Pogge goes to the crux of the matter, to the question of responsibility: "We are involved in an immense crime against humanity, through the upholding of the present global economic order" (RS: a, b, c, d, e, f, g, h, i, j, k).[32] Poverty is imposed through the policies of our elected representatives, non-elected magnates and their unchecked economic institutions, within and across state boundaries. Neoliberalism and its market, a great part of which touts mindless hedonism, has many ways of discouraging reflection on our own responsibility, on how our excessive and trifling consumption choices directly affect the lives of others who are geographically distant, in Congo, for example. Poverty-based human rights violations go back a long way, crossing national boundaries in a historical process whereby hegemony was established by enslavement, colonialism, military conquest, and genocide (RS: a, b, c, d, e, f, g, h, i, j, k, retroactively). Our enjoyment of the spoils of our fathers means ongoing despoliation of other people, mainly third-world dwellers, especially women and children (RS: h). The ethical burden of our present-day generations is to identify, through knowledge of the past, the problems of today and to seek to remedy them. How might a reasonable claim of need against others – the right not to suffer from crippling poverty – become a specifically-designated juridical right that requires specified agents to fulfil legally-prescribed duties aiming at guaranteeing it for everybody? The precondition for the guarantee of universal rights is hinted at in Article 28 of the Universal Declaration of Human Rights, which is more relevant than ever in this era of globalisation: "Everyone is entitled to a social and international order in which the rights and freedoms set forth in this Declaration can be fully realized". Human rights are not just moral claims of individuals on other individuals and their states but, in particular, on the international *institutional* order in which individuals and states function. The problem is that the neoliberal system is not a moral system since it has given preference to The Market over human beings.

On 10 May 1793, Robespierre made the point in strong terms when he said that "the wretchedness of citizens is nothing other than the crime of governments". However, it is not only governments and corporations that are criminals. If we enjoy rights, including the right to know and, forgetting all about duties, we do nothing, we are accomplices in the crime for, as James Baldwin said apropos of segregation and other acts of inhumanity (RS: j, k) in the United States, "It is the innocence which constitutes the crime".[33] We can only show indifference or claim impunity if we resort to pre-Enlightenment primitivism and today, at the beginning of 2013, there are many disturbing signs that suggest that this is exactly where we are heading.

The Verdict

The neoliberal system is guilty of crimes against humanity, as stipulated in the Rome Statute of the International Criminal Court (1998), Article 7 ("Crimes against Humanity"), Part 2 ("Jurisdiction, Admissibility and Applicable Law").

II

Food, Land, Water and the Perishing

In his *Two Treatises of Government* (1689), John Locke (the "father of Classical Liberalism") recognised that, as the product of labour, food was a basic element of property in the development of civil society. However, limits to private property were set by the inviolable rights of all members of society to the earth's bounty:

> All the fruits it naturally produces and animals that it feeds, as produced by the spontaneous hand of nature, belong to mankind in common; nobody has a basic right – a private right that excludes the rest of mankind – over any of them as they are in their natural state: yet being given for the use of men, there must of necessity be a means to appropriate them some way or other, before they can be of any use, or at all beneficial to any particular man. Though the earth, and all inferior creatures, be common to all men, yet every man has a property in his own person: this no body has any right to but himself. The labour of his body, and the work of his hands, we may say, are properly his.[34]

It is only through labour, Locke argued, that human beings can remove something from the common state to which it belonged in nature:

> He has removed the item from the common state that nature has placed it in, and through this labour the item has had annexed to it something that excludes the common right of other men: for this labour is unquestionably the property of the labourer, so no other man can have a right to anything the

labour is joined to – *at least where there is enough,* and as good, left in common for others.[35]

If human products were perishable, he continued, humans were obliged to use them or barter and trade them freely with others before they spoiled. Otherwise they would be wasting the common stock. A man might accumulate baubles but would exceed the "bounds of his just property" by "the perishing of any thing uselessly in it."[36] Money then came into use in the trade between perishable and non-perishable items as "a durable thing".[37] Locke then addresses the relationship of property and the common wealth as a matter of balance and, indirectly, as based on sustainability. One produces but does not waste. One respects everyone else's right to do the same, and cannot appropriate the common wealth:

> As much land as a man tills, plants, improves, cultivates, and can use the product of, so much is his property. He by his labour does, as it were, inclose it from the common. Nor will it invalidate his right, to say every body else has an equal title to it; and therefore he cannot appropriate, he cannot inclose, without the consent of all his fellow-commoners, all mankind.[38]

Locke's account of property in a *civil* society contrasts distressingly with today's uncivilised, ravaged, globalised world, laid waste by the greed of just a few people who *cannot have enough*, thus ensuring that there *cannot be enough* for everyone. People who "inclose, without the consent of … all mankind" exclude themselves from the common run of humanity. In doing so, they also exclude the common people from the common wealth, the means of material existence they need to be fully human. They waste and lay waste in a culture based on "the perishing", and part of that "perishing" today – in the most literal sense – is the waste of people, the horrific category of "surplus population", large numbers of people who stand in the way of the greed of a few. A man or woman "tills, plants, improves, cultivates" the land but is driven off it because some people want to take the land that feeds him or her and the water that quenches his or her thirst so as to accumulate still more of the "durable thing" that will ensure "the perishing of [everything] uselesly" throughout the planet, which is now seriously endangered.

Locke's principles influenced the American Declaration of Independence and are echoed in modern human rights law. Even as the destruction of the earth proceeds apace, the right to food – of all human beings to live in dignity, free from hunger, food insecurity and malnutrition – remains enshrined as a legal right under international human rights and humanitarian law, and under state obligations established under international law. Article 25 of the Universal Declaration of Human Rights and Article 11 of the International Covenant on Economic, Social and Cultural Rights – not to mention a host of other instruments and national constitutions – recognise the right to food. The United Nations Committee on Economic, Social and Cultural Rights states, "the right to adequate food is realized when every man, woman and child, alone and in community with others, has physical and economic access at all times to adequate food or means for its procurement".[39] Following from this definition, the UN Special Rapporteur on the Right to Food, Jean Ziegler, concludes that this entails "the right to have regular, permanent and unrestricted access, either directly or by means of financial purposes, to quantitatively and qualitatively adequate and suffi-cient food corresponding to the cultural traditions of the people to which the consumer belongs, and which ensures a physical and mental, individual and collective, fulfilling and dignified life free of fear".[40]

Ziegler identifies the three As of food justice. It must be *available*, meaning that enough food is produced for present and future generations, which entails the duty of ensuring sustainability and protection of the environment. It must be *adequate*, in terms of both quantity and nutritional quality, to the individual's dietary needs, and also with regard to cultural values and reasonable consumer concerns. It must be *accessible*, meaning that food costs must not jeopardise other basic needs and rights such as health, housing and education, and that all physically and vulnerable individuals have access to adequate food.

The three As of food justice require the state to respect, protect and fulfil these conditions. Under the obligation to respect, states cannot take any measures that arbitrarily deprive people of their right to food; the obligation to protect requires states to enforce adequate laws and take any other necessary measures to prevent individuals or corporations violating the right to food of others; and, under the obligation to fulfil, governments are legally bound to improve people's access to and use of food resources and when, for reasons beyond their control, individuals or groups are unable to feed themselves, states have the duty to ensure they are adequately fed.[41]

International law also enshrines the right to water, thus recognising that a good part of the world's population is in danger of being deprived of such a basic need. By 2007, the High Commissioner for Human Rights had submitted a study to the Human Rights Council in which she concluded that, "it is now time to consider access to safe drinking water and sanitation as a human right, defined as the right to equal and non-discriminatory access to a sufficient amount of safe drinking water for personal and domestic uses – drinking, personal sanitation, washing of clothes, food preparation and personal and household hygiene – to sustain life and health."[42] Several international human rights conventions, including the 1989 Convention on the Rights of the Child (Article 24:1) and the 1979 Convention on the Elimination of Discrimination against Women (Article 14:2), incorporate provisions that explicitly recognise the right to clean water. The most detailed definition of this right was offered in 2002 by an expert body assessing the International Covenant on Economic, Social and Cultural Rights, which only "implicitly" recognizes the right to water. The Committee states: "The human right to water entitles everyone to sufficient, safe, acceptable, physically accessible and affordable water for personal and domestic uses. An adequate amount of safe water is necessary to prevent death from dehydration, to reduce the risk of water-related disease and to provide for consumption, cooking, personal and domestic hygienic requirements."[43]

However, water is not just the essence of life. It crosses borders and therefore has an extraterritorial dimension. It is a source of potential conflict, a political and economic factor. Denying access to water can be used as a weapon. Israel deliberately denies the Palestinians' right to adequate water by claiming total control over shared water resources and enforcing discriminatory policies that prevent the Occupied Palestinian Territories from developing an effective water infrastructure.[44] It is sobering to think that something so basic, so apparently ubiquitous, is increasingly the privilege of the rich. The poor people of the world do not have adequate access to water. The World Water Council estimates that, "1.1 billion people lack access to safe drinking water. 2.6 billion people lack adequate sanitation. 1.8 million people die every year from diarrhoeal diseases, including 90% of children under 5".[45] In one country, 77 million people (about 50% of its population) are suffering from arsenic poisoning because of high levels of arsenic in their ground water. The country is not one of the "developed" countries, of course, because then we would have heard a lot more about the tragedy. It is the "basket case" (Henry Kissinger) of Bangladesh.[46] It is implied, even if no one openly says so, that "basket case" people don't count. Since they are so basic to human existence, food and water and human access to them, point to two basic facts of modern life, before which privileged people are acting like the three (not so) wise monkeys.

1) Enormous surplus populations, of "basket-case" people who are no longer considered human, are fast being created: millions of human beings who simply don't matter to those who call the shots;

2) For these people, our human rights laws and conventions might as well not exist. They would then only have two senses, which would apply to those of us who enjoy basic human rights. Either they can serve as a cynical cover-up for terrible realities or, they can be taken seriously, in which case it is a matter of tremendous urgency to address their failings and introduce institutional mechanisms to guarantee that every single person's basic human rights are respected and that "nobody has a basic right – a private right that excludes the rest of mankind".

Food: A Commodity

Once perishable, food has been turned into a "hard" commodity[47] in a very badly functioning economic system run by fools, to evoke the incisive remark by the Spanish poet Antonio Machado: "Only fools don't distinguish between value and price". Grain is valuable. Archaeology demonstrates that almost all the early human communities stored grain as a cushion for times of war, drought and famine. As late as 1947, when Washington imposed its version of free trade on the industrial nations through its General Agreement on Tariffs and Trade (GATT), the European countries resisted including agriculture as part of the deal and, until the end of the twentieth century, the price of grain was determined in thousands of market places between hundreds of thousands of buyers and sellers. Now it is the benchmark for pricing food and food products.

Shortly after the Second World War, Nelson Rockefeller and a few others of his ilk realised that food could be just another commodity like oil or metals if only the global chain could be organised along monopoly lines controlled by a small group from the same financial elite that was triumphing in other key sectors of the US and international economy. Part of this project was the extraordinarily destructive "Green Revolution", which aimed to create large-scale farming projects around the world, on land where millions of peasants had always made a living. Traditional and national economies were devastated. Newly landless people flowed into the cities and the few who "benefitted" from the "Green Revolution" were thrust willy-nilly into the rapacious global economy, forced to use high-technology products ranging from tractors, to patented seeds, petroleum-based herbicides, pesticides and fertilisers as their water supplies drastically dwindled. By the 1960s, the World Bank had lent its muscle to this project of throttling traditional agriculture in many parts of the world by limiting its loans only to governments that promoted the "high-yielding" varieties of wheat and rice and costly western-produced mechanical and chemical inputs. Temporary spikes in agricultural productivity went hand in hand with drastically lowered water tables and diminished crop diversity, which also thrust farmers into new forms of dependence when they could no longer count on the by-products of the old ways of farming, straw to feed livestock for example. Now they had to buy fodder. Rural credit institutions mushroomed and indebted farmers lost their land but there was no longer any work for landless labourers because they'd been made redundant by mechanisation. Land was more and more concentrated in the hands of the rich.

The next step taken by the new international food oligarchy was to take control of seeds. With the Rockefeller Foundation in the lead, they produced their "own" genetically modified GMO seeds, of two basic types: those that contaminate other seeds with their genes, and "terminator" seeds that are expressly designed not to reproduce. (Inventing seeds that don't reproduce! How perverse is that?) Public and private groups fused to form a powerful cartel that, pushing GMO crops, prolongs the pernicious legacy of the "Green Revolution" by destroying agricultural diversity and using large quantities of dangerous pesticides, with the same beneficiaries and the same social and environmental costs. These groups include the Rockefeller Foundation; the World Bank; the Ford Foundation; the International Service for the Acquisition of Agri-Biotech Applications (funded by the Rockefeller Foundation and Monsanto); the Consultative Group on International Agricultural Research (sponsored by the UN's Food and Agriculture Organization (FAO), the International Fund for Agricultural Development(IFAD), the United Nations Development Programme (UNDP) and, of course, the World Bank); the United States Department of Agriculture (USDA); the United States Agency for International Development USAID; and AGRA, the Alliance for a Green Revolution in Africa, which is co-founded and funded by the Rockefeller Foundation and the Bill and Melinda Gates Foundation. Government funds business. Business funds government. By mid-2012, the agribusiness industry had donated a total of $63,141,411 to US federal political candidates, parties and other political groups, with about 75% going to republicans.[48]

The revolving door spins fast. The United States Department of Agriculture is changing food "safety" rules so that private companies like Monsanto get "speedier regulatory reviews", which is to say less time will be spent on assessing dangers associated with GMOs,[49] for example. Why? Because pared back approval terms mean faster sales and better conditions for competing with countries like Brazil, which has lax approval processes – and never mind the studies that show organ damage and mutations in insects, especially bees. The world's food chain is in jeopardy because 90% of native plants need pollinators in order to survive.[50] In September 2011, by which time GMOs were clearly linked with the decimation of bee colonies around the world in a phenomenon called bee colony collapse, Monsanto bought Beeologics, one of the main international firms devoted to studying bees which, in any case, was already working hand in glove with the United States Department of Agriculture. The giant gene manipulator now controls most of the world's information about bee colony disorder and its relationship with human disorders. In Utah, which has very high autism rates – one in 32 male children – the connection with bees and Monsanto has been made by a doctor who says,

> During critical first trimester development a human is no bigger than an insect so there is every reason to believe that pesticides could wreak havoc with the developing brain of a human embryo. But human embryos aren't out in corn fields being sprayed with insecticides, are they? A recent study showed that every human tested had the world's best selling pesticide, Roundup, detectable in their urine at concentrations between five and twenty times the level considered safe for drinking water.[51]

We can be sure that the United States Department of Agriculture won't be on the case.

Today, the relatively small quantity of grains traded internationally determines the price for most of the grains produced. The GATT Agreement of 1993 introduced conditions for free trade in agriculture. Responsibility for national grain reserves was taken from governments and handed to private companies, namely the US agribusiness giants. Goldman Sachs, JP Morgan, Chase Manhattan and Citibank entered the scene with successive deregulation that put agricultural products on the derivatives markets. Bankers and traders were now at the top of the food chain. The connection between the current food crisis and Wall Street is clear. Between February and June 2008, speculation in commodity markets rose from $55 to $318 billion and, as Frederick Kaufman points out,[52] for "the roughly 2-billion people across the world who spend more than 50 percent of their income on food, the effects have been staggering: 250 million people joined the ranks of the hungry in 2008, bringing the total of the world's "food insecure" to a peak of 1 billion – a number never seen before."

Food prices (which rose by 240% between 2004 and 2011) are, of course, directly affected by the concentration of economic and political power in agribusiness. For example, by 1997 just four companies processed 80% of livestock slaughter in the United States. Three companies control most of the country's dairy products (Dean Foods, Kraft and Leprino Foods). There is only one cooperative (Dairy Farmers of America) to which farmers can sell their milk. One company, Monsanto, controls most seeds in the United States and has a near monopoly on GMO traits. Three companies, Archer Daniels Midland, Bunge and Cargill, have cornered 90% of the global grain trade.[53] This is not just about the United States but about an international market dominated by agribusinesses (many with the support of Washington) as a long-term geopolitical and commercial strategy.

The Bad Economics of Agribusiness

The food produced today doesn't nourish the people of the world. The industry makes sure it doesn't. It snatches food from the mouths of millions to make the mega-rich still richer and is devastating the world's ecosystems. The Consumer News and Business Channel CNBC ("First in Business Worldwide") gives a complacent account of the new food economy:[54]

- … food has become something bigger than itself. It's about far more than sustenance. It's about commodities trading, globalization, trade, energy, biotechnology and government policy.

- Farmers and agribusiness are dependent on government support, even if those policies sometimes hurt consumers.
- Commodities and futures contracts – involving any number of grains, fruits and animal parts – are traded by the millions daily around the world. Rice and cocoa can be more profitable for traders than for farmers or food companies.
- Corn and sugar cane and more are not simply foodstuffs – they are also biofuels.
- Commodities speculation, say some observers, is the major cause of food inflation, which is eating into the pocketbooks of consumers in even the wealthiest countries.
- One thing, however, has not changed [sic – it has changed, and for the worse]: hunger and, worse, starvation, especially in war-torn countries, past or present, such as Angola and Sudan.
- ... government programs to support consumption can make or break a government ...
- Food is also a good barometer of globalization; as incomes rise, more food – and better forms of it –are consumed [by whom?], compounding the supply-and-demand formula.
- Meanwhile, a new generation of entrepreneurs is reversing a decades-long period of flight from the farm [it's called the "land grab"].
- Innovation is also a force, with companies using IT and biotechnology to make crop yields more productive and more perishable [John Locke again].

This economy is making conditions on Earth increasingly precarious for many reasons. The race for land and its resources has taken the form of a direct assault on all kinds of environments – from deserts, to tropical forests, ice plains, scrubland, tundra, savannah plains, thorn forests, wetlands, mountains, rivers, and seas – and the people and animals that inhabit them in the most far-flung corners of the planet. The rush for land is driven by four interrelated factors: 1) the artificial volatility of food prices; 2) the energy crisis and the "solution" of biofuels; 3) the global financial (and geopolitical) crisis; and 4) the new carbon-trading market. All four were crucially important in the 2012 Obama-Romney campaign for the White House because the American economy is badly ailing, with total debts totalling almost $16 trillion in June 2012, and foreign debts of some $5.3 trillion, with China and Japan as the biggest creditor nations ($1.1643 trillion and $1.1193 trillion in US debt respectively), while other creditor nations include Brazil, Taiwan, Russia, the United Kingdom, India, Italy, South Africa and Peru.[55] The western economic model is based on the principles of ravage and waste yet, even with these spectacular figures, very few people are questioning the model itself and the human and environmental toll it is taking. In social terms it is a vile system and in purely economic terms, it doesn't work.

Spiking oil prices over the past decade indicate that this fossil-fuel-based economy can't expand because there are no more energy supplies to meet the demand it has created. Yet it is premised on expansion. So new methods of extracting hydrocarbons in difficult conditions – by fracking, from tar sands, or in the Arctic – are now wreaking even more devastation and all for an economic model in which growth along the lines it has set is impossible.[56] It's worse than bad economics; it's pure madness.

There are hundreds of books and articles detailing different aspects of the destruction of the natural and human world. They aren't isolated instances but each case, distressing enough in itself, is only part of one grossly malfunctioning system. It's very difficult to take it all in. To sum up, we are killing millions of members of our own species, we are bringing about the extinction of many other species, we keep producing weapons that can destroy huge areas of the world, we create greenhouse gases by burning fossil fuels, and we produce chemicals that attack the upper atmosphere which protects us from UV rays. Scientists have identified five "mass extinction events" (when Earth loses more than three-quarters of its species in a geologically short interval) that have cataclysmically reshaped the planet in the past 540 million years. The scientific journal *Nature* suggests that, given the magnitude of known species losses in relatively recent times, a sixth "mass extinction event" might be well underway.[57] The present global economy is destroying the earth's living membrane of animal and plant species as if we were somehow not part of nature, as it if were acceptable that just a few humans and other hardy species – a bunch of mega-rich humans in bunkers with cockroaches to keep them company, perhaps? – should create and survive the next cataclysm.

There are more signs of the catastrophe, none of which appear in economic accounting: the loss of huge quantities of topsoil; eviction of millions of people from land where they once engaged in land and animal husbandry to permit the havoc of large-scale extraction; pollution or emptying of rivers and aquifers; poisoning of the soil and air; deforestation and desertisation; drought, flooding, tidal waves, earthquakes and hurricanes; and the quantities of carbon dioxide being pumped into the atmosphere. The cost will be paid by our descendents, which means that our generation is criminally violating their human rights on an inconceivably massive scale.

Multinational companies talk about "externalities", which are defined as the "uncompensated environmental effects of production and consumption that affect consumer utility and enterprise cost outside the market mechanism". A British consultancy, Trucost, calculates that the "environmental externalities of the world's top 3,000 listed companies, including every company on the Standard &Poor's 500 index, total around $2.2 trillion annually".[58] If "externalities" sounds like an innocuous word, it is because this is a market-oriented calculation that doesn't take human suffering into account, or address the fact that some of these "externalities" arise from places like the Amazon, Kalimantan, Mongolia, Patagonia and the Australian desert, which should have remained outside the "market mechanism" in the first place because the only way they could have been included was through spoliation.

Whatever the ethical issues involved, and human rights are certainly an ethical issue, this is *après-moi-le-déluge* economics, except it will include a lot of drought too. If about half of the hungry people of the world are peasant farmers, what is the sense in taking their land? It certainly has nothing to do with "feeding the world" as the land grabbers claim. Countless studies have shown that industrial agriculture violates just about all the principles of sustainability, which means that the right to sustenance of future generations is wilfully jeopardised as well.

The Food and Agricultural Organisation informs us that world food production could feed almost twice the planet's present population so the problem is not one of production but of access. At the end of the seventies, Somalia, now notorious for its pirates and as a "failed", famine-stricken, "basket-case" state, was self-sufficient in food but the debt repayment policies imposed by the International Monetary Fund and the World Bank in the eighties included the liberalisation of the country's markets and hence a massive influx of non-traditional foodstuffs, for example rice and wheat produced by subsidised western multi-nationals, which then deprived local producers of their livelihood. Food that should be nourishing the world's hungry people is instead the fodder of stock markets to the extent that 75% of financial investment in the world's agricultural sector is speculative,[59] and imaginary wheat dictates the price of real wheat. Industrial food production cannot countenance the rights of small farmers.

The last decade has seen unprecedented investment in the industrial food sector. Farmland, seeds and water are now big business for financiers, pension fund managers, businessmen, oligarchs and Gulf oil sheikhs who, stung by recent experience, want something more substantial than financial bubbles. Global distribution of food is peddled as a top priority. "Everyone needs to eat!" What this really means is that some of us will eat at the expense of others. In any case, land is not only being grabbed for outsourced food production, but also for mining with particular attention to the seventeen superconductive rare earths (97% controlled by China, according to some estimates) which are essential for computers, smart phones, wind turbines, and high-tech equipment like medical scanners, and military uses like stealth helicopters,[60] lasers, and night-vision goggles. There are other interests, too, like luxury tourism, game parks, privately run millionaires' nature reserves, infrastructure, dams, biofuels, timber and carbon trading. Unsurprisingly, a great part of the land being grabbed is in Africa.

Today's newspapers warn of a terrible famine that is about to hit the Sahel region of West Africa, affecting some eighteen million people.[61] Meanwhile global food prices are expected to climb still more steeply thanks to poor crop yields in the United States following the worst drought for fifty years. Climate change is one of the causes of this food shortage in both the Sahel and United States but this, too, is an *economic* factor, the result of bad management of the earth's natural resources, the logical corollary of seeing them not as common wealth to be husbanded in the interests of everybody, but something that excludes the "common right of other men" to be exploited for individual or corporate benefit. It is not just that fuel consumption is one of the main causes of global warming but the "remedy" – biofuels, crops such as oil palm, jatropha, sugarcane and soya – only exacerbates the problem by following the neoliberal golden rule of "more, more, more" (for fewer people). The relationship between biofuels and hunger is more or less quantifiable. "The European commission admits that its target (10% of transport fuels by 2020) will raise world cereal prices by between 3% and

6%. Oxfam estimates that with every 1% increase in the price of food, another 16 million people go hungry."[62]

It goes without saying that the demand for biofuels has exacerbated the massive worldwide land grab, underpinned by claims like the concern to mitigate climate change, or that "green" biofuels are environmentally friendly, or that the "world" needs food. Not only are the old imperial powers involved but also the BRIC nations and what the World Banks classifies as "Middle Income Countries" like South Korea (the world's third biggest importer of corn) and Egypt. Once again, the rights of millions of people in the poor countries are crushed in this modern-day marauding.

The International Food Policy Research Institute (IFPRI) reports that some fifteen to twenty million hectares of farmland were the subject of deals or proposed deals involving foreigners between 2006 and mid-2009.[63] Other estimates are much higher. A World Bank report published in September 2010 revealed that more than 46 million hectares of farmland acquisitions were announced between October 2008 and August 2009 alone, and two thirds of these were in Sub-Saharan Africa.[64] A more recent ILO report states, "The ILC [International Land Coalition] has documented transfers of 80 million hectares from 2008 to 2011", while Oxfam suggests that more than 227 million hectares have been allocated in large-scale land deals since 2001, with the vast majority of those transfers occurring after 2008.[65] The extraordinary variation shown by these figures suggests that this is a very secretive business. If it were as do-gooding as it often claims to be, surely it would be trumpeting its "humanitarian" acquisitions. Something stinks here and it isn't fertiliser. A great crime is being committed and covered up and the international institutions are deeply involved.

Here are some examples (and, for obvious reasons, this account is by no means exhaustive) of recent land deals.[66] South Korea has acquired a total of three million hectares (three times the size of the state of Lebanon, for example) in Russia (500,000 ha), Sudan (700,000 ha), Madagascar (1.3 million ha), Mongolia (300,000 ha), Philippines (100,000 ha), and Indonesia (25,000 ha). China has invested in at least two million hectares in South East Asia (Thailand, Malaysia, Cambodia, and Laos), in Mozambique (800,000 ha), in Russia (80,000 ha), in Australia (45,000 ha), and in Cuba (5,000 ha), Algeria and Zimbabwe, and it was estimated in 2009 that more than a million ethnic Chinese workers had moved to Africa. Japan has acquired a total of one million hectares of land, in the Philippines (600,000 ha), USA (225,000 ha), and Brazil (100,000 ha). India controls a total of 1.7 million hectares in Argentina (600,000 ha), Ethiopia (370,000 ha), Malaysia (300,000 ha), Madagascar (250,000 ha), Indonesia (70,000 ha), and Laos (50,000 ha). Saudi Arabian investors have snapped up one million hectares in Indonesia, half a million hectares in Senegal and 200,000 hectares in Mali, a $100 million wheat and barley farm in Ethiopia, millions of hectares in Sudan and rice fields in Thailand. The Gulf Emirates have 325,000 hectares in Pakistan and another 400,000 in Sudan.

It is impossible to estimate how much land, how much water and how many people and ways of life are affected by this new lust for territory. For one thing, the process is moving so fast. Worse, the people affected simply don't count. Wherever possible, the land is acquired as if it were just a surface (with good water supplies) with no villages, no people, no animals no ecosystems but something that was just hanging around waiting to be exploited. But the villages, people, animals and ecosystems are (were) there. The word "territory" is avoided. "Land" is more neutral in terms of political content and is closer to the idea of private property. The clearest sign that these transactions are far from innocuous is the contracting of armies and militia to protect the newly-acquired "property".

The magnitude of the problem can be roughly gauged from a couple more examples. First, the Saudi government and other

Gulf States are negotiating with Pakistan (where about 80% of the farmers or at least 35 million people have less than two hectares of land or are landless agricultural workers) a contract involving about half a million hectares, in addition to land already acquired. The deal includes the services of a 100,000-man private army to protect the food that will be exported back to Saudi Arabia. Buyers or lease-holders have also been promised legal cover in case a future government in Islamabad is less welcoming.[67] Pakistan, the selfsame state that is evicting the poor from their land, has a Constitution that states in Article 38 (d), "The State shall provide basic necessities of life, such as food, clothing, housing, education and medical relief, for all citizens, irrespective of sex, caste, creed or race, as are permanently or temporarily unable to earn their livelihood on account of infirmity, sickness or unemployment". Shouldn't the government be dismissed for unconstitutional practice? Shouldn't all governments that engage in unconstitutional practices and break international law and agreements be dismissed? They are supposed to be representing and protecting the people.

Home to more than five hundred American Indian tribes, countless species of plants wildlife, insects and micro-organisms for thousands of years, the Alberta (Canada) forest was once a beautiful area with a profusion of lakes, rivers and watercourses that played a crucial role in absorbing carbon dioxide. It is now the world's third-largest oilfield and its oil is extracted from tar sand, a process that is one of the most highly polluting industries mankind has so far managed to invent. Many local people have been relocated to reservations where, bereft of the native soil of their traditions, it is impossible for them to keep their language and culture alive. Surrounded by water, they now have to pay for water in bottles: "Water, water, every where, / Nor any drop to drink". But they weren't the ones who killed the albatross. Needless to say, bottled water is another big industry, mainly controlled by Coca-Cola, Pepsi and Nestlé, *inter alia*. Dirty oil and pure-looking water do mix here as the joint cause of environmental destruction. Production of the bottles (30 billion in the US every year, only 12% of which are recycled) uses 17 million barrels of oil per year and making the bottle takes three times more water than that which fills it.[68]

Oil extraction in Alberta, involving several companies including Shell and Chevron, began in 1967. In recent years, doctors have found a high prevalence of rare aggressive cancers among First Nation communities downstream from the oil fields. An official report by the Canadian National Resources Defense Council on the area of Fort Chipewyan, a remote town in one of the world's biggest freshwater deltas, notes a thirty per cent increase in cancers, a threefold increase in leukaemia and lymphomas and a sevenfold increase in bile duct cancers. The Beaver Lake Cree Indian activist, Crystal Lameman, who is fighting the devastation caused by the oil companies, makes a clear connection between old and new human rights abuses when she says, "They colonised us here. The oil companies are just the last in the line of completely wiping us out".[69] In 2008, the Beaver Lake Cree Nation filed a lawsuit against the Canadian and Alberta governments for permitting the oil companies to destroy their ancestral land. They cited no less than 17,000 violations of their treaty rights.

The mining companies are licensed to use twice as much water as the whole city of Calgary (population 1.2 million) consumes in a year. Each barrel of oil produced requires between two and a half and four barrels of water, but this figure does not take into account wider water and acid rain pollution eloquently attested to in the large numbers of dead and deformed fish reported in the zone. At least ninety per cent of the water directly used to extract the oil ends up in tailing lakes that are so toxic that propane cannons and scarecrows are used to deter ducks from landing in their environs. The poisoned lakes of Alberta cover fifty square kilometres.

Common Land

Common land isn't a thing of the past. The struggles against the seventeenth-century British enclosures were just one instance in the continuing battle for common land all around the world. Even in the large cities of the "developed" world, the same conflict takes the form of citizens' attempts to regain public space, the last form of common, democratic "land" they have. In colonial times, people without written traditions and unprotected by any constitutions or charters, the native populations of North America, Africa, Asia and Australasia, were brutally dispossessed of their traditional lands, murdered if necessary. Then again, there is the terrible toll taken by forced socialist collectivisation in China and Russia, which was anything but what the Diggers and Levellers had fought for, not least because it was based on deprivation of freedom, one of the basic principles of commoning. Seeing the possibilities for their treasuries, colonial regimes intensified the land-accumulating work done by pre-colonial rulers in territorial wars. For example, in what is now Indonesia, it was relatively easy for the cash-strapped (after the Java War and Padri Wars) Dutch to introduce the infamous forced cultivation scheme known as *Cultuurstelsel* (1830-1870) – the "culture system" – which turned much of Java and a good part of the Outer Islands into a giant colonial plantation because, in the name of harmony (nowadays it's called "security"), the early Javanese rulers had already laid the groundwork with their own harsh forms of extracting corvée labour and rice tribute from their subjects. Assisted by the Javanese aristocracy, the literati, and an already-established, mainly administrative, legal system which was based on order and stability, the colonial government forced villagers to pay land rent, to surrender one fifth of their rice fields to cultivate export crops like sugar, coffee and indigo or, in the case of landless peasants, to work in government fields 66 days per year. Famine ensued, of course, and the colonial power became increasingly repressive as armed revolts spread throughout the archipelago.

About ninety per cent of the land – farmland, savannah, woodland, forests, marshlands – in Sub-Saharan Africa is untitled[70] and it is therefore formally under state control. Colonial regimes took advantage of this situation in order to extract resources and use them for their own benefit. The situation didn't change with independence. In many places, local elites simply took over the "rights" the colonial masters had bestowed upon themselves. In traditional society, land was not subdivided and, wherever they could, communities maintained it as collective property, using what they needed to farm while keeping the rest uncultivated in order to sustain the ecological balance of the whole environment, always striving to respect its wildlife and vegetation.

Apart from outright appropriation of land or labour, another colonial ploy was to declare untitled but traditionally occupied common land "*Terra Nullius*" (in the case of Australia, for example) or classify it as "unowned" or "free" land, in which case the state automatically became the legal owner. Today's land grabbers still hide behind spurious laws, frequently international law, or simple decrees from the powerful economic institutions. Hence, the Guinea Savannah Zone, a huge expanse, four million square kilometres of grasslands running through twenty-five countries and almost half the size of the United States, is designated by the World Bank as one of "the world's last large reserves of underused land".[71] In reality, this "underused" land is home to almost one tenth of the world's population, some 600 million African peasant farmers. People don't come into the World Bank's picture of "underused" vast "reserves" that are only waiting to be snatched up by the likes of Monsanto.

Communally owned land, according to traditional or natural law, often takes the form of forests or woodlands, shrublands, savannas, wetlands, grasslands or the Chaco thorn forests which cover two thirds of Paraguay. It adds up to some 8.54 billion hectares or a staggering 65 per cent of the global land area.[72] Human rights violations in these common lands occur on a huge scale and include violent eviction, appropriation, denial of information about deals and contracts, and exclusion of local populations from any decision making.

In Ethiopia, a country which is in the grip of chronic food crisis and heavily dependent on food aid, the Gambella region, bordering South Sudan and representing some ten per cent of the country's agricultural area, has been distributed to Indian, Saudi and other investors. The people have been driven away by threats, attacks, and killings. Among the dispossessed is the shattered community of Anuak farming and fishing people, many of whom are presently herded into refugee camps. The Ethiopian government says it is signing away "empty" land but this is a totally alien concept for the Anuak, who always leave some areas fallow in keeping with the demands of shifting cultivation. Indeed, the high quality of the soil attests to their admirable farming skills. In contrast, when big agribusiness has depleted the soil and dried up the wetlands it will simply move on, as long as there is still land and water to exploit in some corner of the world, but the effects among the remaining local people and their material conditions of existence will be devastating because, dependent on aid and imported food, they lose their farming skills, even if they were able to reclaim their ravaged land. The Human Rights Watch report "Waiting Here for Death: Forced Displacement and "Villagization" in Ethiopia's Gambella Region"[73] details a wide range of grave human rights abuses, from forced displacement, suppressing dissent, arbitrary arrest and detention, physical assault, rape and sexual violence, forced labour, violation of economic and cultural rights, and violation of the right to food security and indigenous land rights. The Ethiopian government, with a view to similar projects, was planning to move 1.5 million people by 2013. At this point, a little comparison won't go amiss. You only have to think of the dramatic press coverage of Hurricane Sandy and the damage it caused on the eastern seaboard of the United States in October 2012 and then wonder why nothing is said about the 1.5 million displaced, traumatised (imagine what it would be like to have all those forms of violence visited on you) people of Ethiopia. The first word that comes to mind is racism. A few people matter and a lot don't.

The other part of the Gambella tragedy is the destruction of the natural world, which of course redounds again on the human world in an ever more vicious spiral. While pastoralism and shifting cultivation have always coexisted in reasonable harmony with wildlife, mechanised farming sees animals – antelopes, elephants, baboons, elephants, buffalos, and so on as a problem – and, in this case, to give just one example, its enclosure of the land blocks the migration of over a million white-eared kob, antelopes that move en masse to the Gambella wetlands at the end of the dry season. Another way of dealing with the wildlife "problem" is to confine the animals in places like the 136,000-hectare Grumeti game reserve in the Serengeti where rich people can have a taste of the wild for about $2,000 per night, plus another $500 to take a balloon "safari" across a part of Africa where "the land stretches forever" (which is the Maasai meaning of "Serengeti"). This particular enclosure is "owned" by the Wall Street billionaire Paul Tudor Jones. Other grabbers of similar large slices of the natural world, now playgrounds for the rich, include Gulf sheikhs, a Mexican-American entrepreneur who charges $22,000 as a trophy fee for shooting an elephant (which is how the "folksy" Spanish king, Juan Carlos I, notoriously likes to amuse himself), philanthropists who want to "save" a slice of the planet and offer "refuge" to those who can pay, aristocrats, a sportswear tycoon wanting to make a "global ecosphere retreat" (for whom?) and so on.[74]

The Water Grab

Water was once common wealth, but not anymore, in particular since 2008 and the onset of the global financial crisis with its extraordinary commodity price spikes and growing financial speculation in food. If there were a way to turn air into a commodity, some financial prodigy would certainly be making a killing with that too. Water, land and resource grabbing intensified exponentially as governments and investors scrambled to find guaranteed returns when The Market became increasingly volatile and unreliable. But investors would have to be the most short-sighted people on the planet, so industrial agriculture was their answer and they also peddled the message that it would solve the fuel problem. (Well, let's say to the extent that it would make immediate profits until planet Earth yielded no more.)

Biofuels squander vast amounts of water in irrigation, washing the harvest, and cooling boilers. One litre of ethanol, the product of twelve kilograms of sugarcane, requires 7,000 litres of water, for example.[75] It isn't surprising, then, to find that recent years have seen the establishment of private investment funds prominently featuring water on their portfolios. But whose water is it? That question isn't asked, as the AgriSar Fund of the Swiss Sarasin Bank makes clear when it states in its prospectus that, "The monetisation of water is just beginning as a previously free asset gains scarcity value and we see opportunities for companies able to secure and manage supply."[76] Take away (give "scarcity value" to) and grab ("secure") what was once a common resource ("free asset") and you'll make a tidy pile ("opportunities"). A "previously free asset gains *scarcity value*" (emphasis added)! Beautiful, clean, soothing water becomes "monetised"! This is the "perishing" of water, the perishing of human communities. How will we drink money?

The water industry is controlled by huge monopolies among which two French corporations, Vivendi and Suez, have "secured" about seventy per cent of the world market. Water is transferred from regions in which it is cheap and abundant, now transformed into food commodities to be consumed in other regions. For example, the European Union "Everything But Arms" (such an ethical sounding name but you might ask what "everything" includes) trade policy, siphons off Cambodia's water for large-scale sugar production and then brings the crop to Europe. The fact that water has traditionally been considered a public good hasn't deterred investors. Water is a "sector", a bankable commodity, a view clearly expressed by Judson Hill of NGP Global Adaptation Partners who told a meeting of commodity traders in Geneva, "There are many ways to make a very attractive return in the water sector if you know where to go".[77] When you think about what it really means, the language of "scarcity value", "attractive return" and "monetisation" of the "water sector" is truly obscene.

Almost all the new land deals in Africa involve large-scale agricultural operations that need huge quantities of water. They are therefore usually located close to major river systems. Elsewhere, the farms pump up ground water. As one investor in Zambia succinctly puts it, "The value is not in the land. The real value is in water."[78] Past experiments with similar irrigation schemes show that they destroy not only livelihoods of rural communities but also the freshwater sources of entire regions. In Pakistan, for example, the British colonisers constructed the world's largest irrigation system to produce the raw material for metropolitan cotton mills. After independence, the World Bank funded an expansion of the system so that what was then the River Indus was eventually used to water ninety per cent of the country's agricultural land, which was by then turned over to "Green Revolution" crops. The price was this:

The Indus carries 22 million tonnes of salt each year, but discharges only 11 million tonnes at its exit into the Arabian Sea. The rest, almost a tonne per year for every irrigated hectare, stays on the farmers' fields, forming a white crust that kills the crops. So far, a tenth of the fields in Pakistan are no longer usable for agriculture, a fifth are badly waterlogged and a quarter produce only meagre crops. Moreover, the water withdrawal is so intense that in many years the Indus no longer flows all the way into the sea.[79]

This model of agriculture that depends on high water consumption generates soil degradation, salinisation and water-logging wherever it is introduced. After "Green Revolution" agriculture in India and China brought on a major water crisis, it is now moving on to Africa, with India and China leading the land grabbers.

Water rights of indigenous communities are subject to customary, collective forms of management and are therefore not registered. Legally "privatising" water resources is a cinch because domestic laws are subordinated to international investment agreements. A 2011 report published by Standard Bank, a Johannesburg-based funder of land grabs makes this crystal clear. International investment agreements "are designed to protect investors, with few of the agreements including any investor obligation, or expressing and recognizing the rights of states to regulate in the public interest." If host countries have few rights in these deals, they must shoulder almost all the oblig-ations so that the investor is entitled *under international law* to draw as much water as deemed necessary, "... even if it conflicts with existing or future needs in local communities for potable water, small-scale farming, small industries or subsistence use".[80] It is hard to imagine a more callous way of saying the human beings in local communities have no rights to their traditional basic means of subsistence when buyers, protected by interna-tional law, want to secure "full rights to crops and land". Still more iniquitous is the fact that, according to the law, the new farmers cannot be banned from exporting food during a famine.

The water factor in the great land grab is illustrated by the case of Saudi Arabia[81] which, surprising as it may seem, once had the world's biggest dairy farm and millions of hectares under heavily subsidised wheat (every tonne of which required between 3,000 and 6,000 tonnes of water, three to six times the global average), but the water was "fossil" water from an underground reservoir up to four thousand feet deep, a finite resource. Now that it is running dry, Saudi Arabia (together with other Middle East countries) is outsourcing agriculture in heavily subsidised deals favouring its water-depleting farmers and buying or leasing land in Sudan, Ethiopia, Mali, Mauritania, Niger, Senegal, Nigeria, Egypt, Vietnam, Cambodia, West Papua, the Philippines and Pakistan. Meanwhile Qatar has done land deals in Vietnam, Cambodia, Uzbekistan, Senegal, Kenya, Argentina, Ukraine, Turkey, Tajikistan, Australia and Brazil. One thing can be taken as given: these investors will not be worrying about water conservation in the host countries. In Australia, for example, water being sucked up from ancient aquifers is being touted as "new water".

The nexus of food, water and multinationals came together in the remote village of Plachimada, Kerala, India, where a $25-million Coca-Cola bottling plant dried up local wells only months after it began its operation in 2001. Shortly afterwards, tests carried out at the University of Exeter in Britain showed that the leftover sludge was laden with heavy metals, especially cadmium and lead, and already contaminating the food chain. This sludge was being distributed by the company to farmers as "free fertiliser". Cadmium is a carcinogen which causes kidney damage, while exposure to lead causes mental derangement and death and is particularly dangerous for children, causing severe anaemia and mental retardation. Professor John Henry, a leading toxicity expert and consultant at St Mary's Hospital in London, warned of "devastating consequences for those living near areas where this waste has been dumped and for the thousands who depend on crops produced in these [paddy] fields".[82] Worse, the New Delhi-based NGO Centre for Science and Environment (CSE) found in 2003, "that nearly all colas and 'mineral water' produced in India contained unacceptably large doses of commonly-used pesticides".[83] The Kerala State Pollution Control Board ordered the closure of the plant in 2005 but no criminal action was taken against the company for its serious crimes of taking the villagers' livelihood and knowingly poisoning their fields and hence the people.

International law makes local users invisible, redundant, less than human. Private investment rights are highly visible and protected. How does that mesh with the Universal Declaration of Human Rights? Who makes the law and for whom? A National Security Memo 200, dated April 24, 1974, and titled "Implications of World Wide Population Growth for U.S. Security and Overseas Interests", tells us how Henry Kissinger envisaged the highest priority of U.S. foreign policy towards the Third World:[84]

Whatever may be done to guard against interruptions of supply and to develop domestic alternatives, the U.S. economy will require large and increasing amounts of minerals from abroad, especially from less developed countries. That fact gives the U.S. enhanced interest in the political, economic, and social stability of the supplying countries. Wherever a lessening of population pressures through reduced birth rates can increase the prospects for such stability, population policy becomes relevant to resource supplies and to the economic interests of the United States.

Kissinger recognises that "mandatory programs" of population control might be needed and asks, "Would food be considered an instrument of national power? ... Is the U.S. prepared to accept food rationing to help people who can't/won't control their population growth?" Food "rationing", in Mr. Kissinger's view, can "help" some people so others can grow fat. And what exactly does he mean by this externally imposed "population policy"? Starvation is a very effective method of population control.

A Tiny Minority (as anti-universal as you can get)

Evidently, when human rights abuse is committed on such a scale the perpetrators hide their names and faces – no problem in the great big globalised world. The states of origin of corporations are less visible, for example, than international institutions like the World Trade Organization and some of the agreements that shield them. While it is convenient and to some extent accurate to take up the Occupy slogan and speak of the 1% who are trampling on the rights of the 99%, most of the 1% are wannabes by comparison with the most ferocious enemy of universal human rights, which is what David Rothkopf (former managing director of Kissinger Associates) calls the superclass.[85] According to Rothkopf, the superclass, is 94 per cent male, mostly white, from Europe and North America, and numbers between 6,000 to 7,000 people, or the approximately 0.000001 per cent of the world's population which sets the agendas at Davos, the Trilateral Commission, Bilderberg Group, NATO, G-8, G-20, the World Bank and the World Trade Organization. From the stratospheres of government, military headquarters, NGOs, finance capitalism, transnational corporations and academia, these are the people who decide, along Kissingerian lines, who will and who will not have water. They are latter-day Molochs for whom whole populations are sacrificed. If more than 24,000 people, 14,000 of them children, die of hunger or hunger-related diseases every day because of the demands of the superclass, then each of its members kills someone, most frequently a child, every six hours.

In June 2012, managers of pension funds and hedge funds met in London at a highly elite £3,660-a-head "Agriculture Investment Summit" to discuss investment opportunities (and how to "overcome perceived obstacles to investment") in buying up swaths of land in Africa, "one of the greatest investments in the world".[86] It would seem that many western investors agree. Land Matrix,[87] a public database of land deals, shows that seventy million hectares of arable land, or five percent of the continent's land mass, have been sold or leased since 2000. British companies have the rights to more than 3 million hectares, which represent two-thirds of the UK's total farmland. Land Matrix[88] also estimates that, since 2008, some eighty-two million hectares of land, which is to say 1.7 per cent of the world's agricultural space has been snapped up in poor countries by new developers. Since precise data and ownership details are deliberately obscure, the figure is likely to be much higher. The local impact – eviction, sometimes at gun point, of whole communities of peasants, hunter-gatherers, herders, and fishing people who are dispossessed of their means of subsistence, permanent termination of food production, water depletion and massive destruction of ecosystems – was never as much as "perceived". The "obstacles" were more to do with getting round the law in different countries but, when it comes to investment and when it is well greased, law can be wonderfully supple.

This situation is what Franz Neumann warned of six years before the Universal Declaration of Human Rights was promulgated, and he wasn't only talking about National Socialism: "As a device for strengthening one political group at the expense of others, for eliminating enemies and assisting political allies, law then threatens the fundamental convictions upon which the tradition of our civilization rests."[89]

Protecting the Right to Food

The right to food is as basic as it is complicated. It is inextricably bound with the economic environment, both local and global. A small spike in food prices on the stock exchange can tip many of the world's communities into famine, while the accumulative effects of low agricultural production in local communities can cause prices to shoot up around the globe. A large number of international factors affect the right to food. In recent decades, structural adjustment programmes imposed by international financial institutions have removed price controls, eliminated government spending on feeding the poor, and cancelled food and agricultural input (fertiliser and pesticide, for example) subsidies, all of which has caused sharp increases in food prices. The imposition of cash crops like coffee, palm oil and cocoa have only added to a vicious circle of fluctuating prices on the inter- national market, difficulty in debt repayment, devaluation, extreme price hikes and increased poverty.

The transnational corporations, benefitting from structural adjustment programmes, are increasingly engaged in production of out-of-season fruit, flowers and vegetables for sale in the markets of rich countries. A plethora of studies in the wake of the 1960s Green Revolution has demonstrated that cash crop production destroys local ecosystems and dramatically reduces biodiversity by eliminating thousands of traditional plant varieties when patented seeds are imposed by the multina- tionals. It is not as if we are short of evidence. Food security is threatened because the genetic pool for higher-yielding and more pest-resistant crops is dramatically reduced. Pesticides encourage the appearance of new, resistant pests and viruses. Forests, with their great variety of animal and plant species, are being cut down for rubber, tobacco, coffee and palm oil, and the land, devastated by soil erosion, is unfit for local food production after the transnational companies extract all they can and then move on from the now-dead soil. Other activities of transnational companies such as overfishing and resource extraction cause great damage including crude-oil contami- nation of crops, land and water in rivers and lakes, destruction of agricultural activity, depletion of fish and shellfish stocks, usurpation of water supplies, air pollution, often in the form of acid rain, which spreads the damage much further afield, and species extinction. Water is a crucial factor since it is privatised in such a way that farmers cannot use it for irrigation and then the right to food is doubly affected since safe drinking water is evidently essential to adequate nutrition, apart from being crucial in food production.[90]

Transnational companies are notorious for labour abuse and failure to pay a living wage to their workers, a situation which is exacerbated by their extraordinarily concentrated power in the agricultural sector and hence over inputs and outputs. Consumers in developed countries are also affected as fresh local produce that is not grown from genetically-modified seeds or treated by pesticides and fertilizers (which contain undisclosed substances) is increasingly difficult to find.

The food-related practices of international institutions and transnational companies amount to nothing less than Crimes against Humanity, as defined in the Rome Statute of the International Criminal Court (1998), Article 7 ("Crimes against Humanity"), Part 2 ("Jurisdiction, Admissibility and Applicable Law"). These crimes pertaining to the right to food arguably include murder; enslavement; deportation or forcible transfer of population; severe deprivation of physical liberty in violation of fundamental rules of international law; persecution against any identifiable group or collectivity on political, racial, national, ethnic, cultural, religious, gender or other grounds that are universally recognised as impermissible under international law; enforced disappearance of persons; the crime of apartheid; and other inhumane acts of a similar character intentionally causing great suffering, or serious injury to body or to mental or physical health.

It may be easier to point the finger at transnational companies – aided and abetted by legal systems – as food criminals than it is to imagine the most powerful governments in the world deliberately engineering a crime against humanity based on denial of food to an entire population. It happened and they got away with it. The evidence was submitted in the British parliament and nothing happened. The killers are still on the loose and still wielding power. Carne Ross, the senior British official responsible for the imposition of sanctions in Iraq, stated before a parliamentary select committee in July 2006, "The weight of evidence clearly indicates that sanctions caused massive human suffering among ordinary Iraqis, in particular children, and equally massive damage to Iraq's economy and civilian infrastructure, damage for which Iraq is still paying today. We – the US and UK governments who were the primary engineers and defenders of sanctions – were well-aware of this evidence at the time, but we largely ignored it or blamed all these effects on the Saddam government. ... [We denied] the entire population the means to live ... forcing them into dependence on UN and government-supplied rations."[91]

Yet, besides the duties of each state *vis-à-vis* its citizens, agreements with the international financial institutions (IFI) and a number of international declarations and conventions, in particular the International Covenant on Economic, Social and Cultural Rights (ICESCR), supposedly respect and protect the right to food. The relationship between national and international rights and obligations is clearly pointed out by Smita Narula:[92]

> States Parties to the ICESCR are obligated to ensure that the right to food is respected and protected in IFI agreements. It further proposes that home states must exercise due diligence in regulating the activities of TNCs [transnational corporations] where it can be shown that the home state exercises decisive influence over the ability of TNCs to operate in an unregulated manner abroad. The due diligence and decisive influence standards have been shaped and defined by international law jurisprudence.

Narula notes that social and economic rights have low status in a human rights milieu that, for obvious reasons, mainly monitors and promotes "first generation" rights, in such a way that any possible development of customary human rights law is adversely affected. For example, the United States has not ratified the International Covenant on Economic, Social and Cultural Rights, was the only country to vote against the UN resolution on the right to food[93] and, indeed, opposes the right to food as a legal obligation. Narula points out that while some Universal Declaration of Human Rights (UDHR) norms have become customary international law, for example the right to be free from slavery and torture, the sequence of events leading to and following the adoption of the UDHR raises doubts as to whether *all* of its norms can claim such status. "It is therefore necessary to determine whether, apart from the UDHR, evidence exists pointing to widespread state practice and *opinio juris* supporting the treatment of the right to food as customary international law." This evidence would seem to exist, she says, in human rights treaties (for example Article 11 of the ICESCR, which clearly specifies the right to food); humanitarian law (for example the Geneva Conventions which stipulate that prisoners of war must be supplied with adequate food that the occupying power must ensure that the occupied population has food and medical supplies); United Nations resolutions (for example Resolution 57/226, *The Right to Food*,[94] which states that "food should not be used as an instrument of political or economic pressure" and endorses "the right of everyone to have access to safe and nutritious food, consistent with the right to adequate food and the fundamental right of everyone to be free from hunger so as to be able fully to develop and maintain their physical and mental capacities."); resolutions imposing sanctions also recognise the right to be free from hunger as a fundamental human rights norm,[95] even though this right was notoriously ignored with the sanctions imposed on Iraq after 1990; declarations (for example that of the 1996 World Food Summit held by the Food and Agriculture Organization (FAO) of the United Nations and the Millennium Development Goals, signed by every country and every international body, the first of which calls for the eradication of extreme poverty and hunger); and constitutional rights.

On the basis of all of these treaties, resolutions, declarations and constitutional provisions, Narula concludes that, "A particularly strong argument [...] can be made that the right to be free from hunger has already achieved the status of customary international law."[96] Further steps must now be taken to include the broader right to adequate food in this status.

Economics talk and human rights talk take place on separate planes yet it is glaringly evident that economic growth can only guarantee food security for everyone if it guarantees human rights and works towards poverty reduction and eradication. Human rights make no sense at all if adequate nutrition and food security are not included and duly protected as basic rights. The rights-based approach refers to government obligations, in both national and international spheres, to ensure that people are free from hunger, which obviously means that they must have access to adequate food. *Laissez-faire* economics rides roughshod over international human rights law, which is premised on the notion that states must intervene to respect, protect, and guarantee the right to food. Article 11 (2) of the International Covenant on Economic, Social and Cultural Rights, which encompasses two separate but related norms, the right to be free from hunger and the right to adequate food, states that parties to the Covenant

... shall take, individually and through international co-operation, the measures, including specific programmes, which are needed:

(a) To improve methods of production, conservation and distribution of food by making full use of technical and scientific knowledge, by international cooperation and the realization of human rights disseminating knowledge of the principles of nutrition and by developing or reforming agrarian systems in such a way as to achieve the most efficient development and utilization of natural resources;

(b) Taking into account the problems of both food-importing and food exporting countries, to ensure an equitable distribution of world food supplies in relation to need.[97]

States, then, are theoretically obliged to (1) respect the right to food by non-interference with existing access to adequate food; (2) protect food supplies by ensuring that individuals are not deprived of access to adequate food by other individuals or enterprises; and (3) guarantee the right to food by engaging in activities that are intended to strengthen people's access to and utilisation of resources and means to ensure their livelihood, including food security and, moreover, the State is obliged to provide the right to adequate food whenever an individual or group is "unable, for reasons beyond their control, to enjoy the right to adequate food by the means at their disposal."[98] The millions of people who continue to suffer and die from hunger or hunger related illnesses testify in the most tragic way not only to the failure of the international "community" (another tragically debased word which, *de facto*, in realpolitik terms of international power, refers to the "superclass") to respect the "right to food" in its supposed "fight against hunger" – and how is it possible, one might ask, to fight against hunger without respecting the right to food? – but also the ineffectiveness of international law in protecting the basic rights of the vulnerable, and its great effectiveness in making their exploitation possible. Yet, as Narula makes clear, the right to food is both hard law and a strong moral imperative, unless we want to be completely impervious to the plight of our fellow humans.

Almost sixty percent of the approximately thirty-six million annual deaths worldwide are a direct or indirect result of hunger and nutritional deficiencies or infections, epidemics or diseases which attack the body when its resistance and immunity have been weakened by undernourishment or hunger.[99] Over ninety-five percent of the world's malnourished people live in the "developing" world. Hunger is the tightening stranglehold of a vicious circle in which hungry workers produce less, earn less, eat less, are hungrier and weaker and thus more likely to fall ill. Malnourished mothers have sickly children who, if they survive, suffer physical and mental damage, do poorly at school and are therefore ill-equipped to work and produce. If sustained, equitable economic growth is one antidote to hunger, ending hunger guarantees a healthier more productive population and is therefore a key strategy for ensuring the economic health of a country. However, combating hunger is not just a question of national production figures but of each person's moral entitlement within the overall food supply of the economy. Now the economy is on a global scale.

The overall result of all the different kinds of land and water grabs is that more and more people have been stealthily dumped on the "perishing" pile. These "surplus" populations are herded into "villages" (villagised), as in Ethiopia, or displaced into refugee camps, decimated by poverty, famine, disease and war and, if they ever make it to cities, used as tools in dehumanising work, in sweatshops, as sex workers, baby machines for the adoption market, or organ providers. Some of the effects are appearing in the developed world too as people lose their jobs, are pushed out of their homes, and are obliged to eat unhealthy or insufficient food. More and more people are sleeping rough in the world's most prosperous cities and when you sleep rough you eat rough, often on pickings scavenged from rubbish bins. This is a completely deranged situation. Food, a basic human need and something that is so beautiful when shared, is now a compelling indicator of how degraded human society has become. The words of Yeats' poem "The Second Coming" describe the situation in which the plant, animal and human world is now floundering:

Things fall apart; the centre cannot hold;
Mere anarchy is loosed upon the world,
The blood-dimmed tide is loosed and everywhere
The ceremony of innocence is drowned.

How can we stop the "perishing"? How can we stop things – human society – from falling apart? The only way we can make the centre hold is to call upon what we share, our shared humanity, what we have in common. Food, once the symbol and reality *par excellence* of shared production and consumption, the essence of social existence, has now become a shatterer of social life, an extremely antisocial source of wealth, a weapon ("instrument of national power") against any living creature that gets in the way of profit. The system that has brought about this situation is criminal, depraved, a sociopath. When a person is hungry it means that he or she has been stripped of all the other trappings of social life. This is a sub-human existence and those who are responsible for it are also less than human, and in a much worse way. The "rough beast", which "Slouches towards Bethlehem to be born", is our own creation. We can only stop it by trying to be *truly human*. That means reclaiming and protecting every single person's human rights, in our own practice and with legal instruments that befit a *truly human* society. Some of these are already in place, supposedly protecting (to quote Jean Ziegler again) "the right to have regular, permanent and unrestricted access, either directly or by means of financial purposes, to quantitatively and qualitatively adequate and sufficient food corresponding to the cultural traditions of the people to which the consumer belongs, and which ensures a physical and mental, individual and collective, fulfilling and dignified life free of fear".

We need to think hard about what kind of world we should have in order to guarantee these conditions, and compare it with the cruel and destructive system we have now. Then, if we prefer Ziegler's just world, we must insist on the real implementation of these rights and ensure that those who offend against them are stopped and punished. Reparation paid by the "superclass" would go a long way in the "fight against hunger", but the essential condition for winning the battle is a social system that respects human rights and that introduces every policy instrument that is necessary to protect them, starting with guaranteeing material existence. Before that, however, we must recognise the present problem as it really is. If we accept words like "underused land" from people who really mean they are going to clear people ("perceived obstacles" to investment) off it, we will never be able to demand justice because we won't know what it is.

III

The Human Rights Lexicon

Extremely dangerous ground, which requires the most scrupulous prudence and caution, language also constitutes a fundamentally antagonistic, powerful weapon. [...T]he art of oratory in ancient China is identified with the art of war and of strategic intelligence.[100]

Half a millennium before the Common Era, Confucius was warning of glib men and their empty words as the Warring States period was evermore dominated by silver-tongued orators, mercenaries of the word, which is to say the equivalent of today's spin doctors. The great sages of those long-ago times repeatedly pointed out that orators who use words as an instrument of persuasion, weapons cynically detached from their proper context and sense, denying any reality they may originally have denoted, were at the root of all the evils and misfortunes threatening the nation. In Book 13 of the *Analects* Confucius describes a clear chain of events leading to social disaster. If language is twisted, what is said is not meant, so what must be done is not done. If what must be done remains undone, morals and justice are undermined and, without justice, the people are thrown into confusion. There can be no social contract if the words for constituting the contract are suspect for one can be sure then that the state of the nation is not what it is said to be. When the words representing the values and ethics of a society are stripped of their real meaning, we should be alarmed for the health of the reality they are supposed to convey. Twisted usage alone tells us that something is being concealed. Let us not be bamboozled or lulled into inaction by false, a-historical use of words. Recognising that words have history, revealing their past so as to shed light on the present, understanding what has been stripped from them and appreciating their original poetry, is a fecund and even revolutionary endeavour.

In a recent case, in his speech after the assassination of Osama Bin Laden in Abbottabad, Pakistan, by US Special Forces, the former law professor, US President Barack Obama, proclaimed on 2 May 2011, "We will be true to the values that make us who we are. And on nights like this one, we can say to those families who have lost loved ones to al Qaeda's terror: Justice has been done." Perhaps the lawyer Obama was ignorant of the axiom *nemo esse iúdex in sua causa potest* (nobody can be the judge of his or her own cause). In any case, whatever happened that night – entering another country's space to execute an unarmed man, shooting him in the head in front of his family, killing up to five other people, then hastily and secretly dumping the body at sea – it wasn't justice, which necessarily entails due process of law, a fundamental, constitutional guarantee that all legal proceedings will be fair in a properly established court, with a formal prosecution, a defence, a hearing of the evidence, and a judgement, all in strict accordance with the law. Yet hardly anyone noticed that justice, too, had been assassinated. American citizens danced and waved flags in the streets of Washington and New York, and the victory was hailed by the sly words of statesmen. The British Prime Minister David Cameron thought it was a "massive step forward" (to what?), the Foreign Affairs Ministry of India called it a "victorious milestone" while, for the Israeli Prime Minister Benjamin Netanyahu, it was a "resounding triumph".

The hunting down of Bin Laden, this "resounding triumph", has taken a toll of almost one and a half million dead in Iraq,[101] more than 10,000 civilians killed in Afghanistan, over 7,000 troops of the occupation forces in Iraq and Afghanistan sacrificed, and a total cost of the so-called "War on Terror" approaching 1.4 trillion dollars.[102] After the execution of Osama Bin Laden, President Obama concluded his victory speech declaring, "We are once again reminded that America *can do whatever we set our mind to*".[103] With a claim like that, no wonder the grammar is faulty. In the same speech he extols "the story of our history", "the pursuit of prosperity for our people", "the struggle for equality for all our citizens", standing up for "our values abroad", and US sacrifices in making "the world a safer place."

Obama's "story of our history" slips smoothly over the harsh facts of a nation built on genocide, slavery and racism. It was no accident, or at least one of those Freudian slips that reveal stunning truths, that one code name for the Abbottabad operation was "Geronimo", taking "the story" back to some kind of Wild West "justice", like the gunfight at O.K. Corral. Geronimo (Goyaałé, "one who yawns"), a legendary warrior, famous for his valour, strategic skills and eluding US and Mexican authorities, was part of a long tribal history, the struggle of the Chiricahua Apache against Spanish settlers, and Mexican and US soldiers who were stealing their land. If *we set our mind to* insinuating that Bin Laden is an ancient enemy of the kind that was vanquished in the foundational myth of America (the true story being that victims, who were only an "enemy" because they didn't want to relinquish their ancient lands, were annihilated rather than vanquished in any battle that observed the laws of war), just one word, the name of a bad-guy Apache, does the job.

President Obama says America "can do whatever we set our mind to". In that case, poverty rates estimated at 14.3 percent of Americans in 2009, and a US child poverty rate (20%) that is second worst among the rich nations, and an infant mortality that is the worst, haven't entered the mindset. So, how can he talk about "the pursuit of prosperity for our people" and "the struggle for equality for all our citizens"? Thirty-one million Americans are estimated to be unemployed or underemployed (2012) and the unemployment rate for African Americans is double that for white jobless people. If America is not setting its mind to these enormous social problems at home, what "values" does President Obama think he's spreading abroad? It's more than likely that the political demise of Bin Laden was definitively sealed with the uprisings that began in the Arab world four months before his death, but this was a victory that had to be snatched from the Arab people and replaced with the message from the O.K. Corral.

If *just* (from the Latin *justus* or "upright", "impartial" and "equitable", and also *jus* meaning "right" and especially "legal right" or "law") can so easily be torn from justice and taken back to a racist founding myth of America in which the cowboys (at the time, often deemed to be outlaws) won by gun power, "human rights" have suffered a similar fate in being stripped of both "human" and "right". One only needs to recall George W. Bush's claim in 2004 that, "No president has ever done more for human rights than I have".[104]

In recent years we've seen all the attempts at convincing the world that Saddam Hussein had weapons of mass destruction, or that water-boarding isn't torture and that George W. Bush is the world champion of human rights. American presidents talk a lot about human rights. George W. Bush, the president who defended torture, rendition of prisoners to the world's darkest dungeons, water-boarding, Abu Ghraib, Guantanamo and suspension of *habeas corpus*, was also the president who was known for his public howlers so we could assume he meant to say, "No president has ever done more *to* human rights than I have". However, Bush's grasp of prepositions is one thing and his contempt for human rights, which he reveals in his arrogant and patently untrue assertion, is quite another. It's not the grammar but the contempt that matters. Whatever rights he's talking about – and one gets an inkling with a glance at his self-conferred "right" to suspend other people's rights with his (262!)[105] executive orders, including crippling the pro-transparency Presidential Records Act (13233), sidestepping the

Geneva Conventions (13440), bringing back secrecy by withdrawing declassified documents (13292), enabling all kinds of abuses in Iraq (13303 and 13438), and tampering with federal regulations on environmental policy in favour of big business (13422) – they are not *human* rights. Bush's notion of "right" is a cornerstone of neoliberalism, the kind of right that's equated with might, and he certainly did his bit for that. Since the term "human rights" has been so traduced by the powerful, a Manifesto that claims human rights in the terms in which Mohamed Bouazizi understood them will need to go back to the radical beginnings, to the real meanings of the words.

Universal

"[A]ll moral philosophy may as well be applied to a common and private life, as to one of richer composition: every man carries the entire form of human condition."
- Michel de Montaigne, XIV, "Of Repentance", *Essays*, 1580.

A right is not an arbitrary or unfounded pretension. It is "an expectation that adduces reasons and arguments, that is deemed to be 'well-founded', 'legitimate' or, if one prefers, 'just'."[106] In theory, the generalised nature of a *human* right distinguishes it from any privilege confined to a group, class or caste and hence the emphasis on "universal" in modern declarations of human rights.

In the globalised psychology of today, universal reach is the privilege of the rich and powerful. They're even booking their tickets to travel to outer space in 2013. Intrusion from other parts of the globe is the lot of the poor and weak. Rich global consumers, see universality reflected in the menus of their favourite restaurants[107] which give a loving account of the exact origins of the ingredients in their premier dishes where they can savour Kumamoto oysters, English peas, Nantes carrots, Piedmont hazelnuts, Madras curry, Périgord truffle, San Marzano tomatoes, and Sicilian pistachio, and so on. This lotus-eating geography reveals how the real geography of the world's countryside is being concreted into one gigantic global shopping centre in which a carrot can't be appreciated as such but, for the rich, must come with a pedigree. This is the complacent consumer's view of universalism we are fed.

In the most famous human rights document of modern times, the United Nations Universal Declaration of Human Rights, the positioning of the adjective is revealing. The adjective "universal" qualifies not human rights but the Declaration itself. In a globalised age, anybody can make a "universal" declaration with the aim of reaching everybody. This Manifesto could be "universal" too inasmuch as it is addressed to everybody but the much-needed universality of human rights is not about audience numbers, which is something more associated with short-lived events like the funeral of Princess Diana, which apparently had the biggest global audience ever. "Universal", in the sense of this Manifesto, must always be bound with two other words: universal+human+rights. Obama can declare to the whole world that America "can do whatever we set our mind to" but this is arr(og)ant blather. Achieving universal application of the Declaration's contents is quite another matter, well beyond speechifying with words that are now so void of real meaning that they are routinely suspect. As soon as one becomes a human being "in general", in the rhetorical "universal" sense, one is deprived of human rights because this conjectural figure has no citizenship, no place in the real social and economic structures and power relations that shape everybody's life.

The word "universal" may be a commonplace in human rights talk but its ordinariness doesn't stop it being an obscene affront to all the millions of people who, without access to the basic means of existence, can't exercise their human rights. According to World Bank figures for 2005, some 1.37 billion people were then living on less than $1.25 a day, 2.56 billion on less than $2 a day and 5.05 billion (more than 80% of the world's population) on less than $10 a day.[108] The poverty analysts Thomas Pogge and Sanjay Reddy estimate[109] that the number of poor is almost fifty per cent higher than the World Bank figure.[110] If they can't even get the sums right, so that they know what the problem really is, the most powerful institutions of the developed world aren't taking poverty seriously, as the cloud-cuckoo-land title of one World Bank report would also seem to imply: "The Developing World Is Poorer Than We Thought, But No Less Successful in the Fight against Poverty." The other enormous gap, of course, is that which yawns between the very rich and the very poor. Extreme poverty is concentrated in war-prone states and territories with fragile institutions, deficient policies and refugee crises and they account for almost thirty percent of the world's desperately poor people. A quarter of the developing world's population (85.4% of the desperately poor), some 1.14 billion people, are living without sufficient means for *human* survival.

Somehow, we're supposed to think there is some real basis for what Article 2 of the United Nations Universal Declaration of Human Rights (1948) declares:

Article 2
Everyone is entitled to all the rights and freedoms set forth in this Declaration, without distinction of any kind, such as race, color, sex, language, religion, political or other opinion, national or social origin, property, birth or other status.

Furthermore, no distinction shall be made on the basis of political, jurisdictional or international status of the country or territory to which a person belongs, whether it be independent, non-self-governing or under any other limitation of sovereignty.

The Declaration is a document of valuable and legitimate aspirations. It wasn't drafted with hypocritical or obscene intentions beyond, perhaps, shoring up the shining Cold War image of the United States as the "Land of the Free" in contrast with the dark realms of the Communist world. The essential problem – which makes one suspect that image is all-important in this document – is that it offers no mechanisms that might implement and guarantee human rights. In it, human rights are deemed to be the entitlement of "humans" in general, as if they could be distributed to "everyone", an abstract entity, a mass of humans divorced from social, economic, political identities and relations, especially class relations, as if they were not the birthright of individuals – every single individual – who live in different societies and whose lives are governed by particular social and institutional structures. This excision from the real world of social, economic and political relations means that human rights become little more than an arbitrary dispensation emanating from power relations, the hot air of grand utterance.

The uses of human rights, now travestied as humanitarianism in a globalised world shows how the supposed defence of human rights has turned into its perverse opposite. One illustration will suffice: one of the Pentagon's "8 objectives of war" in Iraq was "to immediately deliver humanitarian relief, food and medicine to the displaced and to the many needy Iraqi citizens".[111] The logic of this seems to be, first create "the displaced" (many into graves) and then give the survivors humanitarian alms. In this regard, the *casus belli* meets the household-word aspects of human rights halfway, to the extent that many people wouldn't express opposition to a "humanitarian" cause, which they understand as helping others, especially the vulnerable, tragic children who are so often used in the images of humanitarian money-raising publicity. As the Pentagon planners were well aware, talking about what seemed to be human rights in another part of the globe seemed a much more acceptable reason for going to war than Saddam Hussein's non-existent "weapons of mass destruction". Human rights have been demoted to humanitarianism, which is in large part a tool of late-twentieth-century imperialism or, in certain ideological and instrumental respects, a latter-day version of the "civilising mission" of the colonial era, which takes us back to the "human-itarian" King Leopold II and his genocide in the Congo. It's hardly surprising, then, that human rights are now being used as a pretext for violating international law and national sovereignty.

There are many examples that support the assertion that human rights, in the form of humanitarianism, have become just another instrument of universalising neoliberalism. It's clear enough in the undisguised words of a powerful neoliberal, reported by *Agence France Press* on 18 January 2005, just after the tsunami that devastated Southeast Asia and took some 300,000 lives, "I do agree that the tsunami was a wonderful opportunity to show not just the US government, but the heart of the American people, and I think it has paid great dividends for us". The speaker is the then Secretary of State designate, Condoleezza Rice. The "great dividends" come from the economic foothold afforded by aid "donations" – with huge profits for businesses in the "donor" countries – arbitrarily and temporarily doled out to the right-less victims of war, famine, drought, and natural or man-made disasters, to people *en masse* whose lives are reduced to bare survival and stripped of civic dignity because they don't have the material means to exercise their rights. The world's poorest people are in a similar permanent "humanitarian disaster" situation. This description doesn't only refer to "accepted" disaster zones such as Haiti, Afghanistan or Darfur, but increasingly to the United States itself, where the polarisation between rich and poor is such that some analysts are starting to talk of "debt peonage".[112]

The universal reach of today's militarised neoliberalising "human rights" is patent in the thinking of the Office of the Coordinator for Reconstruction and Stabilization, U.S. Department of State (S/CRS). In its declared mission of helping "societies in transition from conflict or civil strife" to "reach a sustainable path toward peace, democracy and a market economy", one of its main strategies is to "Deploy Humanitarian, Stabilization, and Reconstruction Team (HSRT) to Combatant Commands to participate in post-conflict planning where U.S. military forces will be heavily engaged".[113] The military overtones are also crystal clear in a speech made by the then Secretary of State Colin Powell as far back as 2001 when he described NGOs as "such a force multiplier for us, such an important part of our combat team."[114]

Apart from what is presently occurring in Iraq and Afghanistan – the violence, the suffering and the bonanza for United States construction and weapons companies[115] – humanitarian missions, from Honduras, Guatemala and Nicaragua after Hurricane Mitch, to Aceh, Thailand, and Sri Lanka after the tsunami, to Cambodia and the more recent post-humanitarian disaster, East Timor, all show the dismantling of local systems and the dire consequences of that as these economies are pulled into the neoliberal systems and their economies are reshaped (bloated by inflation), although the word employed is the euphemistic "reconstruction". As Shalmali Guttal from Focus on Global South says, "It's not reconstruction at all – it's about reshaping everything."[116] Universal in the neoliberal sense means "can't be local".

The Cree Indians point out that only when the last tree has died and the last river poisoned and the last fish floating belly up will we realise we can't eat money, but this is not the economics of Wall Street bankers and the industrial-military complex. The application of what the Pentagon calls "force-multiplier" human rights in neoliberal projects is what Naomi Klein calls "disaster capitalism". Her coinage describes the rapaciousness but doesn't identify the other disaster, which is the undermining of human rights and what they are supposed to stand for.

A further problem of universality in the case of human rights is their division into different classes, as if they were independent of each other. In the West, where human rights purveyors tend to have no problems with their material conditions of existence, mainstream discourse gives priority to individual and political rights. This is well-illustrated by the sneering attitude of the former United States Ambassador to the United Nations Jeane Kirkpatrick when she described economic and social rights as "a letter to Santa Claus".[117] It's true that the 1948 Declaration offered a unified conception of human rights but it wasn't long before they were torn asunder by the International Covenant on Social, Economic and Cultural Rights[118] and the International Covenant on Civil and Political Rights.[119]

This division was exacerbated by the now-freely-used notion of "generations". Following the much-cited and influential scheme proposed in 1950 by T. H. Marshall,[120] which was modified at the end of the 1970s by the Czech jurist Karel Vasak,[121] "first generation" rights have come to mean civil and political rights, protecting the individual from excesses of the state (freedom of speech, right to assembly and to a fair trial, et cetera). Those of the "second generation" social, economic and cultural rights are concerned with equality (expressed in employment, social security, health care and so on), while the wide-ranging, ill-defined "third generation" rights are essentially international and collective (including self-determination, social and economic development, and the right to natural resources). This focus on separate "generations" made possible the blithe obscenity of the words of the former Spanish prime minister, José María Aznar who, in March 2008, described the situation in Iraq as "… not idyllic but it is a very good situation."[122]

Some thinkers have insisted that the different kinds of rights are important and mutually reinforcing. For example, Amartya Sen famously observes that, "No substantial famine has ever occurred in any independent and democratic country with a relatively free press"[123] and – putting the cart before the causal horse – that real social and economic development can only occur in poor countries when there is greater freedom of choice for all members of society.[124] However, the prevailing view is that of clear-cut "generations", this false hierarchy of rights and suggested independence of spheres which have obscured the need to identify and focus on the right upon which all others rest: the right to the material means of existence. In a nutshell, the formal, artificial excision of political rights from their material conditions of enactment has systematically obliterated poverty as a human rights concern.

If the word "universal" refers to a declaration of rights *to* everybody it is just hot air. If it is *for* everybody, then human rights are radical since this implies equality, fraternity and freedom for every single person on the planet. However, the qualifier "universal" is logically redundant because "human" is a universal category. A name more in keeping with present human rights practice would be "Universal Declaration *to* All Humans That Human Rights Are *for* Some Humans". If a member of the human species is to be "human", as the word has generally been understood since the Enlightenment, he or she must enjoy the rights that make the *human* condition possible. These rights are deemed to be *universal* on the assumption that, as the hypothesised offspring of our Most Recent Common Ancestor, our East African forebear known as Mitochondrial Eve, all humans share a single gene pool that distinguishes them from other species. It is generally agreed that, in order to be operative or, better said, real, the rights qualified by the adjective "human" require human dignity and freedom which, in turn, are based on the fundamental condition of the right to material existence. Nobody can dispute the obvious but frequently ignored truth that, "Without life, no other value is sustainable".[125]

Human rights, even the most basic rights, are NOT universally enjoyed. It is a falsehood to suggest that the fully "human" condition is universal when rights are being trampled underfoot by securocrats who speak of "dark forces", the "axis of evil", "terrorist nests", non-human figments of deranged imaginations, from which the "free world" must be protected. Neither is this "free world", which must be made "secure" (for whom?), human. It is The Market. Apart from the instrumental fantasies creating this crazed Manichaean world of some humans and the rest, there is the allied tragic real-life fact that the inhuman conditions of existence of almost half of humanity reduce them to being sub-human or people who can't fully exercise human powers.

Human

Let's start with what humans aren't. We're not just nodes in a virtual "social" network, however much some nerds and geeks would like to believe we are. We're sentient beings and, however sanitised online *noli-me-tangere* relations might beguile us into forgetting this fact and all the complications it entails, we can't escape from Shylock's question, which applies to every single human being: "If you prick us, do we not bleed?" Too many people are bleeding, suffering, starving, dying and too many have information about this but are not sentient enough. How is it possible to address and redress the abasement of our humanity in the Information Age? Universal human rights, with emphasis on each word, are one possibility. This requires knowing what human rights are and claiming them for everybody, an endeavour that can only be radical in form and effect.

Of course the social media can be used to this end but real, sentient, human, beings and their dignity and freedom must always be the foremost concern if they are to be effective in upholding, defending and trying to achieve guarantees of universal human rights. The online "social" network is not real-world society. The former is, in fact, confined to the privileged few in worldwide terms. According to WikiAnswers (2012) only 21.1% of the world's population has access to a computer. It goes without saying that these users are concentrated in the wealthier countries. In one virtual form of human interaction, software becomes an intermediary between people, encouraging swift, superficial contacts in an activity consisting of exchanges of mindless trivia. Called "friending" (with a one-click "remove a friend" option), it has lost the old sense of *befriending* (making and being a friend) in being shrunk to instrumentally *doing* friendship. It is often related with trying to expand business networks. No lesser maven than Jaron Lanier, pioneer of virtual reality and an early leading light of *Wired* magazine has this to say:

> The whole artifice, the whole idea of fake friendship, is just bait laid by the lords of the clouds to lure hypothetical advertisers—we might call them messianic advertisers—who might someday show up.[126]

With devices like Facebook and Twitter, anybody can "do" a thousand "friends", an impossible feat in real life, but the form of communication with them could not be expected to go much beyond "tweets" (prattle, babble, chatter, gabble, jabber, yap, blether, yak, yabber, witter, rabbit, chunter, waffle – animal sounds). Friending has nothing to do with the origins of the word "friend", which has the much deeper and more committed connotations of "to love" and "to favour" (from Old English *freogan*) and it is also related with "free" (Old English *freo*). Language is debased. So is life itself when it is presented as an online database of the reduced persona of *virtual* reality. Mere information can never reproduce the whole person. Worse, the persona presented online can be completely false, as many a gullible romance seeker has discovered after being stripped of the family fortune. The reality deficit appears especially poignantly in the messages a murdered teenager's friends post: *"Sorry babes! Missin' you!!! Hopin' u iz with the Angles, I remember the jokes we used to have LOL! PEACE XXXXX"*.[127] It is as if they have no idea of a real person and the tragic end of that person.

Twitter affords a good example of the ambivalent benefits of quick-serve ubiquitous information. A random selection of ten #humanrights tweets from September 2012 and the information yielded by the links they offered reveals the enormity and complexity of both the tremendous drama of old and new (but always interconnected) human rights violations around the globe and the challenge of digesting and acting on so much apparently disperse information. How does our *human*ity respond? Anyone working in the field of human rights knows that denouncing and opposing abuse of any kind in any corner of the globe is all-absorbing. If you are concerned about genocide in West Papua you can't devote time wondering what to do about femicide in Ciudad Juárez,[128] however sick it makes you feel. You just don your human rights blinkers and focus on your own job. Yet human rights abuse can't be corralled into neat sub-headings. As a *human* problem it can only be addressed as a whole because the abuses are all connected. And the victims, as humans, are related with us, the lucky non-victims. The task is daunting, as demon-strated by the ten random tweets shown below but, paradoxi-cally, the human focus condenses it to a single more or less manageable question and a passionate one too as it points to a much better world: what does a human being need to be fully human?

The answers lie in the Universal Declaration of Human Rights, however deficient it is: respect for human dignity, which neces-sarily entails freedom and justice, and the conditions that will guarantee them in the realm of political economy, which is also the lowest common denominator linking the great variety of human rights abuses. However, what also emerges from this and any other sample of #humanrights tweets is that law and order, supposedly social mechanisms to protect the rights of citizens, actually work against them in the interests of a tiny minority. If we know how to shift from the micro to the macro and see the general situation in its particular aspects then we'll also see the need to address the global economic system and the legal institutions and measures that enforce it while purporting to protect human rights.

#humanrights 1. Thirty-four mineworkers in the Marikana mine in North West Province of South Africa were killed on 16 August after police opened fire on them using automatic rifles and pistols.[129] Those in power who gave the police permission – encouraged them – to use live ammunition will probably not be brought to justice because the Constitution is based on the protection of private property and the police were just "doing their job".

#humanrights 2. Water scarcity resulting from government timber-harvesting policies (in favour of whom?) and the concomitant deforestation, which results in reduced rainfall, is fuelling "inter-ethnic" wars in Kenya.[130]

#humanrights 3. The US Marines and Army have violated rule of law in subjecting the whistleblower Bradley Manning, who exposed military crimes, to cruel and degrading treatment in prison. The UN Special Rapporteur on Torture, Juan Mendez concluded in his report on the treatment of Manning following his arrest in May 2010 that, "imposing seriously punitive conditions of detention on someone who has not been found guilty of any crime is a violation of his right to physical and psychological integrity as well as of his presumption of innocence".[131] Meanwhile, known war criminals, torturers and murderers go unpunished. For example Marine Staff Sergeant Frank Wuterich, who ordered the 2005 Haditha massacre that killed 24 innocent Iraqis (including children), did not go to jail and none of the Marines who carried out the killings were prosecuted.[132]

#humanrights 4. The Los Angeles Police Department (LAPD) regards journalist photo shoots in "public" spaces as suspicious activity, sufficient for the police to file a report, open an investigation and forward any further information about a suspect to the federal authorities. The files are sent into a Consolidated Crime and Analysis Database (CCAD) which can eventually end up at the LA area's Joint Regional Intelligence Center, where other intel is interpreted, dissected and divulged by agencies like the FBI and the US Department of Homeland Security.[133]

#humanrights 5. The U.S. Africa Command (Africom) was created in 2008 (to command what?). Since then, *inter alia*, the Pentagon has established a base in Djibouti, in the Horn of Africa and intervened with NATO in Libya. The resulting instability has now spread to Mali. The Pentagon has deployed drones in Somalia resulting in the deaths of hundreds of nationals and – ostensibly to prevent piracy – there is a huge Pentagon and EU naval presence off the coast of Somalia in the Gulf of Aden, one of the most lucrative shipping lanes in the world. Somalia has been identified as a major source of oil reserves and Canadian, British and US firms claim to have purchased oil concessions there. The Obama administration also announced that 100 Pentagon Special Forces and advisors were being dispatched to Uganda, Central African Republic, South Sudan and the Democratic Republic of Congo (DRC) to track down Joseph Kony, leader of the Lord's Resistance Army (LRA). Uganda is another oil producing state, as is South Sudan while the DRC is a rich source of strategic minerals. This oil-fuelled activity is just the tip of the iceberg as African land and water resources are also valuable commodities in the eyes of powerful multinational companies.[134]

#humanrights 6. The western installed and supported Al Khalifah dictatorship that has ruled Bahrain since "independence" continues its crackdown on protestors and #humanrights advocates. This appalling situation occupies very little western news space. Supporters of the regime fear that #humanrights unrest in Bahrain could ignite an explosion in Saudi Arabia – and hence an interrupted oil supply – amongst the Saudi Shi'ites who have long suffered at the hands of the extremist Wahabi Sunni Al

Saud regime installed by the British decades ago. At stake nowadays is the USA's ability to control one of the world's critical choke points, the Straits of Hormuz where the Persian Gulf meets the Indian Ocean.[135]

#humanrights 7. In Sudan, women who challenge racism, religious and ethnic discrimination and call for peaceful coexistence among the Sudanese people, are prosecuted and subjected to sexual violence by Sudan's security service. In Darfur, the Nuba Mountains, the Blue Nile region and elsewhere rape is used as a weapon by government forces.[136]

#humanrights 8. On 28 August 2012, Judge Oded Gershon of the Haifa District Court dismissed the civil lawsuit brought on behalf of Rachel Corrie's family against the State of Israel for the unlawful killing of their daughter. Corrie had legally entered Gaza and was living with Palestinian families in Rafah trying to help them defend their homes which were threatened by demolition by the Israeli Defence Forces. Corrie, a proponent of non-violent activism, was crushed by a bulldozer but, in the Haifa court, was found guilty of her own death – she should have "removed herself from the situation" – by a legal system that has enabled the occupation for almost fifty years.[137]

#humanrights 9. Western meddling in the Middle East is an old story and the consequences today are dire. Nearly fifty years ago, for example, Britain and America plotted an anti-Soviet "regime change" in Syria, which was seen to be an obstacle to petroleum supplies. In 1957 Harold Macmillan and President Dwight Eisenhower approved a startlingly frank CIA-MI6 plan to, *inter alia*, fund a "Free Syria Committee", stir up the Muslim Brotherhood, instigate an internal uprising by the Druze, stage fake border incidents with operations in Jordan, Iraq, and Lebanon, and blame them on Damascus, in order to provoke an invasion by Syria's pro-western neighbours. In the absence of support from other Arab countries, the plan was eventually shelved. Yet it sounds very familiar today.[138]

#humanrights 10. Apart from the "War on Terror" another "simulated war" is the "War on Drugs" which is really a means of managing the global drug trade in which the "Narco-Industrial Complex", including big banks and finance groups in Europe and the USA – for example, Bank of America, Barclays, Citigroup, Credit Suisse, HSBC, ING and Wachovia – are pocketing the profits. Big money is involved. According to the United Nations Office on Drugs and Crime (UNODC) in its *Estimating Illicit Financial Flows Resulting from Drug Trafficking and Other Transnational Crimes*,[139] "If only flows related to drug trafficking and other transnational organized crime activities were considered, related proceeds would have been equivalent to around US$ 650 billion per year in the first decade of the new millennium, equivalent to 1.5% of global GDP or US $870 billion in 2009 assuming that the proportions remained unchanged. The funds available for laundering through the financial system would have been equivalent to some 1% of global GDP or US$ 580 billion in 2009." Naturally, "the 'interception rate' for anti-money-laundering efforts at the global level remains low. Globally, it appears that much less than 1% (probably around 0.2%) of the proceeds of crime laundered via the financial system are seized and frozen." Why? The former UNODC director Antonio Maria Costa offered one explanation in 2009, stating that "the proceeds of organised crime were 'the only liquid investment capital' available to some banks on the brink of collapse .... [and] a majority of the $352bn (£216bn) of drugs profits was absorbed into the economic system as a result."[140] Indeed, America's wars on "terror" and "drugs" are effectively the same, contributing towards creating para-states of semi-official (police and paramilitary) terror in Colombia and Mexico and bringing about a major increase in drug production in Afghanistan. Peter Dale Scott points out that "the overall pattern that drug production repeatedly rises where America intervenes militarily – Southeast Asia in the 1950s and 60s, Colombia and

Afghanistan since then [and] ... Opium cultivation also increased in Iraq after the 2003 US invasion ... And the opposite is also true: where America ceases to intervene militarily, notably in Southeast Asia since the 1970s, drug production declines."[141]

These ten apparently unrelated items posted on Twitter give a desolate picture that can be viewed from many perspectives. Perhaps most sobering is that of law and order, which supposedly protects human rights, but as soon as we start asking questions – like why? how? for whom? against whom? and how much? – it takes us directly into the terrain of political economy. These tweets tell us that forces of law and order around the world kill workers who protest for better conditions; break their own laws in punishing anyone who reveals that they are breaking the law; are paranoid about citizens filming in public spaces, which is exactly what governments do in their mad surveillance of whole populations; occupy the continent of Africa in the guise of bringing "peace" in order to secure mineral resources, land and water, thus triggering off "inter-ethnic" wars over basic needs; support, with silence and arms, regimes that maim, kill, torture and imprison any of their people who protest against generalised repression; systematically rape women who call for human rights; kill human rights defenders and then blame them for their own deaths; plot to sow chaos in the resource-rich Middle East; and foment terror and nourish the drug trade in purported wars against both.

If law enforcement is inhuman, as these tweets show, it necessarily treats huge numbers of people as sub-human. People who are forced to be "sub-human" in the real world are in thrall to conditions of poverty or subjugation that annul all possibility of freedom. One is hungry, cold, sick, weak, in pain, excluded, despised, tortured, deprived of liberty, silenced and, accordingly, stripped of the human "nature" that supposedly distinguishes our species. The ethics and values that are the glue of human "society", a word of old meanings bound up with higher feelings, are also bereft of sustenance when dire poverty becomes chronic. From around 1500, society was taken to mean an entity characterised by friendliness or "friendly association" while, in its Latin adjectival sense (*socialis*), it signifies "united" or "living with others", which is related with "companion" (*socius*, in Latin, *secg* in Old English and *seggr* in Old Norse). From the early eighteenth century it meant "liking, or liking to live with others, disposed to friendly intercourse". Nowadays the word is often cynically accompanied by the adjective "civil" (from the Latin *civilis*, relating to a citizen, public life, what befits a citizen, with a *social* sense of courteous, considerate manners, as opposed to the rough ways of soldiers), as if there were one homogenous body called "civil society" in which everybody is a citizen.

Extreme conditions of prolonged bare survival prevent humans from being "human". A woman who survived the Warsaw ghetto weeps when she watches Yael Hersonski's documentary *A Film Unfinished*. In the ghetto she had become impervious to seeing corpses lying around like rubbish. Watching the film, she cries. "Today [...] I am human. Today I can cry again. I am so glad that I can cry and I am human."[142] In his study of the Ik people of the Kidepo area of northern Uganda, hunter-gatherers until the area of their sustenance was declared a national park and they could no longer survive from the land, Colin Turnbull[143] describes how their society disintegrated when they were forced into a confined, settled existence in a harsh mountain terrain that didn't cover their survival needs, and permanent scarcity turned their existence into the barest subsistence, the harshest struggle for survival. They stopped caring for their old people and even their children. Their religious beliefs disappeared, their values were reduced to one, *ngag* (food), "the prime maxim of all Ik being that each man should do what he wants to do, that he should do anything else only if he is forced to" (p.152).

[T]here simply was not room, in the life of these people, for such luxuries as family and sentiment and love. [...] The children were as useless as the aged, or nearly so; as long as you keep the breeding group alive you can always get more children. So let the old go first, then the children. Anything else is racial suicide, and the Ik, I almost regret to say, are anything but suicidal. (pp. 108–9).

For those positive qualities we value so highly are no longer functional for the Ik; [...] they spell ruin and disaster. It seems that, far from being basic human qualities, they are superficial luxuries we can afford in times of plenty, or mere mechanisms for survival and security. Given the situation in which the Ik found themselves [...], man has not time for such luxuries, and a much more basic man appears, using much more basic survival tactics. (p. 27).

Globalised neoliberalism continues the work of undermining the condition of being human, of the "social animal". As Mike Davis puts it, "The late-capitalist triage of humanity [...] has already taken place."[144] All the people who can't be incorporated into the production process have become a redundant, anonymous mass: surplus population. We know the names of a lot of the rich of the world and see their mansions, fleets of cars and other trophies in glossy magazines, but the poor, the excluded, those human beings comprising the great mass are nameless. Their status as a largely undifferentiated multitude is hard to associate with human features, values and rights, even in the most basic aspects of everyday existence. Mike Davis cites an aid worker's description of an apparently humdrum situation that is really the ultimate logic of neoliberalism in a context of "absolute immiseration".

Now everything is for sale. The woman used to receive you with hospitality, give you coffee, share all that she had in her home. I could go get a plate of food at a neighbour's house; a child could get a coconut at her godmother's, two mangoes at another aunt's. But these acts of solidarity are disappearing with the growth of poverty. Now when you arrive somewhere, either the woman offers to sell you a cup of coffee or she has no coffee at all. The tradition of mutual giving that allowed us to help each other and survive – this is all being lost (p. 184).

In these cases, the shedding of ethics, justice, generosity, hospitality, the sentiments of love and friendship, and of community are the result of conditions of bare survival (or as one Baghdad slum dweller said, "semi-death"[145]) forced upon people in Warsaw by the Nazis, in Uganda by a government that gave higher priority to the animal inhabitants of Kidepo than to its human ones, in a ravaged Haiti and in all the places where the great global land and water grab is now occurring. Policies of the strong that demote some humans to sub-humans are no rarity in history. Today's neoliberal policies are doing the same.

If the absolute value for the Ik was *ngag*, that of the new overlords is money. The Ik were not free to choose how to live. The powerful apostles of *laissez-faire* do choose, in the name of extreme and evermore concentrated "freedom" (for The Market), "liberty" that throttles the other two Enlightenment values of equality and fraternity which, if *human* is to be truly universal, must temper freedom. In his book *The Power of the Dog* – a novel, not an academic and still less a government-funded study and hence more credible – Don Winslow describes the functioning of the "Mexican Trampoline", the trafficking of cocaine from Medellin to Honduras to Mexico and to the United States, the flow of arms in the opposite direction and the collusion between the Mafia, Mexican drug lords and the American government. The pillars of the business are voracity and betrayal. The richer the drug barons get, the richer they have to become to pay hired killers to protect their wealth. Every law is broken in the process.

No crime is too bestial. Highlighting this fact, one famous Mexican drug lord called himself "*Mata Amigos*" (Friend Killer). Not only rival males are horrifically tortured and murdered but also women and children. Torture can only grow in savagery and the "human" imagination is put to the task of inventing evermore fiendish torments, supposedly to discourage rivals, although there would seem to be pleasure in it too. The only way the bosses and their thugs can prove they are men is through the bestiality of their behaviour. Nothing but money is sacred, trust disappears and betrayals move ever-closer to home until brother finally betrays brother. It is Ik-in-opulence and, this time, it is voluntary. There are many other examples of this present law of the jungle, which is no place for humans.

One of them is the proliferation of slavery, sometimes coming under other names like chattel slavery, bonded labour, human trafficking, forced labour, and forced marriage. This abominable condition that proclaims the inhumanity of the abuser and the sub-humanity of the abused is not only alive and well but big business today, as any discerning Google search will show. It is estimated that there are some twenty-seven million enslaved people today, compared with twelve million at the height of the transatlantic trade. Three out of four are female and half are children. Today's slaves come cheap, their value set at an average of some $90 compared with (today's equivalent) $40,000 for a slave in the American South. At this low price they are dispensable, replaceable and disposable. There is no need even to provide them with salubrious living conditions.

The most widespread form of slavery is medieval-style bonded labour, servitude demanded as repayment of a debt or loan, which thanks to the cyclical nature of debt and work can mean lifelong bondage. Some slaves are forced to work by armed guards, often slaves themselves. In 2005 the annual profits of human trafficking, mainly for forced labour and sexual slavery, were estimated by the International Labour Organisation at

$US31.6 billion. This makes it one of the top three highest-grossing criminal industries along with arms and drug trafficking. In its *Global Report on Trafficking in Persons* (2009),[146] the United Nations Office on Drugs and Crime, gives a breakdown of annually trafficked persons: men 12%; women 66%; children 22%. Moreover, millions of people – more than half of city-dwelling Indonesians, 60-70% of Central Americans, some 65% of the populations of Dhaka and Khartoum, and 75% of Karachi – subsist in the so-called "informal sector" which, far from being an alternative economy in which entrepreneurial spirits can triumph with a bit of microcredit here and there, is a feudal-style inferno of no contracts, no rights, no regulations, no bargaining power and all manner of forms of exploitation, abuse and exclusion in which humans, and especially women and children, scrabble to stay alive (or "semi-dead") today, and whether they work tomorrow is often a matter of the whim of some gang, criminal or militia leader.

Human? The word originally comes from the Latin *humanus* and is related to *humus* meaning "earth" and earthly beings, as opposed to gods, all more or less equal by virtue of that fact.

Rights

As an adjective, "right" can be traced back to the Greek *orektos* (stretched out, upright), the Latin *rectus* (straight, right), Old Persian *rasta* (straight, right), Old Irish and German *recht* (Law), while the Welsh *rhaith* and Breton *reiz* mean just, righteous or wise. In its everyday modern political sense, it means the opposite of left (radical), which is to say conservative (conserving what?) or reactionary. This is precisely the way in which our de-radicalised human "right"s are understood and wielded today. Like State-based political systems that are supposed to protect citizens, they have lost all credibility. As a verb meaning "to right", the word radically links up with the *legal* aspects of rights through the Old English *rihtan* (straighten, rule), the Old Norse *retta*, the German *richten* and the Gothic *garaihtjan* (straighten) and, as a noun, with the Latin *rex*, the French *roi*, the Spanish *rey*, the Catalan *rei*, with derivatives like adroit, meaning skilful (and human rights, as crudely wielded by the powers-that-be today, are anything but this). *Rex* originally referred to a commander, a president, harbouring the ideas of guide and direct (*regere*) and that of the moral, and perhaps fiduciary, sense of *rectus* (which then takes us to *correct*). In the Indo-European languages, the root is *reg* which, as a noun, means true and powerful guide. In particular, we have the Spanish *derecho* (from the Latin *directus* and of Indo-European root *reg*), meaning law, which is supposed to be a binding practice or custom of a community, and this again comes back to the fiduciary sense of caring for the members of the community by means of establishing rules (back to *regere* again) to protect against abusive excess by any individuals.

There is nothing right about the neoliberal system. It is morally wrong and wrong, too, in the sense of being the opposite of right economics (from the Greek *oikonomia* – household management thrift – and related with *oikonomos* – manager or steward, a word that comes back again to the fiduciary sense of public trust and confidence). Instead of good public management, it has unleashed the lords of chaos and destruction on the planet. In the words of Pankaj Mishra,[147]

The hope that fuels the pursuit of endless economic growth – that billions of consumers in India and China will one day enjoy the lifestyles of Europeans and Americans – is as absurd and dangerous a fantasy as anything dreamt up by al-Qaeda. It condemns the global environment to early destruction and looks set to create reservoirs of nihilistic rage and disappointment among hundreds of millions of have-nots – the bitter outcome of the universal triumph of Western modernity, which turns the revenge of the East into something darkly ambiguous, and all its victories truly Pyrrhic.

Yet, the governing institutions uphold the system as "right" and impose it everywhere. Wrong is right and the present notion of rights is wrong.

One of the world's villages, Bil'in in the West Bank, is a microcosm of the macro-situation in which, when it comes to rights or what is right, everything is topsy-turvy. Israel's biggest IT company, Matrix, has "outsourced" its activities, exploiting very low-paid, ultra-orthodox women living in state-subsidised settlements of the Occupied Territories and opening a new centre called Talpiot – after the Israeli Defence Forces' elite combat unit, thus making allegiances ultra-clear – in the fast-growing settlement of Modi'in Illit. In this rabbi-supervised, kosher site, the women workers, many of them mothers of large families, are extremely disciplined and obedient. The rabbis repeatedly use the term *gezel* (meaning to take by force and robbery) to refer, not to the land that has been snatched from the local inhabitants, but to women who steal their employers' time by chatting on the job.

The settlement itself has received the "Beauty Star Award" (sic) from the Council for a Beautiful Israel (sic) for its impeccable appearance. Its sewerage flows into the Modi'in stream, polluting the water of the entire area. The wall guaranteeing "security" (and generating fear) for the settlers has taken 455 acres of the Bil'in farmers' land, thus depriving them of their livelihood, even though the Israeli Supreme Court decided in the villagers' favour in 2007. Nonetheless, the route for the wall was chosen at the insistence of real estate developers with housing projects valued at some $230 million, so money won the day – illegally. The Bil'in villagers have been organising rigorously peaceful weekly protests for some six years. Many people have been injured, some critically, and two have been killed by the Israeli Defence Forces. Peaceful protest by owners disenfranchised by the land grab is righteous but illegal in the "democracy" of Israel. One of the leaders of the demonstrations, Abdallah Abu Rahmah, spent more than a year in prison after being found guilty of organising an exhibition of ammunition used against the protestors and charged with "possession of Israeli arms" and incitement. That's how insane the system is.

Another aspect of the insanity is that there has been almost no protest from the Israeli public. The academic establishment has been very quiet about all the abuses in the almost half-century of the occupation. It is certainly not outstanding for its defence of universal principles of human rights, not even in self-interest although this is a system that contaminates and harms Israelis too. A new book called *Occupation of the Territories. Israeli Soldier Testimonies 2000 - 2010*[148] demonstrates further perversion of language. "Prevention" by the Israeli Defence Forces, supposedly defensive action against terror, becomes aggression against civilians in order to create a generalised feeling of persecution, achieved by means of violent house searches, fake arrests of Palestinian civilians as practice exercises for young soldiers, incessant armed patrols, and humiliation, harassment and contrived delays at checkpoints making any freedom of movement all but impossible. What exactly are they "preventing"? The Israeli soldiers, and the population at large, come to see this kind of abuse as routine and then, thanks to inertia, as right, since it is so embedded in the system. One soldier says, referring to fanatical settlers in Hebron,

> [Palestinian kids, aged eight and fourteen] ... die for no reason, innocent, where settlers go into their homes and shoot at them, and settlers go crazy in the streets and break store windows and beat up soldiers ... and lynch the elderly, all these things don't even make it to the media. ... [The settlers] do what they want and the soldiers are forced to protect them. ... People prefer not to know and not to understand that

something terrible is happening not far from us, and really no one cares. And the soldiers there are unfortunate and the Palestinians are super-unfortunate. And no one helps them (p. 373).

This young soldier could be talking about the world in general. He understands the system enough to comment "you are a sacrifice yourself", pointing out that it can be universal in the warped sense of not distinguishing between human beings in situations when the rule becomes "anybody can be sacrificed" (even though, in general, it is highly discriminatory). This habituation to evil can by no means be described as "banality". It is huge, part of a thoroughly wrong worldwide system that runs according to its own rules and that is oblivious or hostile to the moral decisions of individuals, including lawmakers. It requires the apathy, indifference, and ignorance of ordinary people to permit the racism, violence, lies, thuggery, savagery, voracity and everything wrong that it presents as right. Of course rights can't thrive in a system of generalised passivity. The only way we can put right back into rights is for everybody to take up the cry, to demand them, to show what is really wrong and insist on what is really right.

Over the last sixty years "human rights" have morphed into everything from a household word to a *casus belli* (the "humanitarian intervention") and there is great disagreement as to what they actually are. This suggests that something is very wrong with the concept. If human rights were universally practised they would be understood from Arnhem Land to Zug. Instead, they are used selectively for many a political purpose by those privileged with human rights, often in the name of others whose alleged human rights are supposedly being protected even while they are being abused. The result is a double bind: no theory = no practice / no practice = no theory.

Human rights have been sequestered and de-radicalised,

lifted and severed from a context that is radical and deep, precisely because they are *human* and thus universal. If we are to have human rights, in any authentic sense, they must be restored to their origins in the words that name them, to the true nature of their universalism, to the sense of "belonging to all", and as the logical and moral claim that all humans should be able to make to and for all other members of their species – just as the Universal Declaration of Human Rights proclaims.

Dignity

Another conceptual problem related with the idea of universality of rights is the concept of human dignity, an old and honourable notion with some interesting etymological roots. The Latin *dignitas* is a derivative of *dignus*, meaning worthy and which, in turn, seems to come from *decnus* meaning suitable, proper or fitting. It is also related with the Sanskrit *daśasyati* (he seeks to please, shows honour or is gracious) and this sense of graciousness and hospitality is also found in the Proto-Indo-European word *dek* which adds a dimension of reciprocity of sentiment since it means "to accept, receive, be suitable". In this respect, dignity also has the meaning of an absence of degradation, humiliation, insult and other unsuitable forms of violence. This may be a philosophically complicated concept but almost anyone knows that his or her dignity at least depends on the absence of abuse by other people and this implies a certain innate sense of equality before, if not the law, some notion of justice: nobody has the right to infringe on my dignity.

Although philosophers had been grappling with the concept for centuries without coming to any widely agreed-upon conclusions, the language of human dignity made a radiant but tragically-tinged entry on to the stage of modern politics as the founding principle of modern human rights with the United Nations Charter of 1945, a document that stated in its Preamble that "WE THE PEOPLES OF THE UNITED NATIONS [...]

reaffirm faith in fundamental human rights, in the dignity and worth of the human person [...].[149] This avowal was a heartfelt response to the terrible crimes against humanity and human dignity perpetrated during World War II but the conceptual foundations were shaky. The explicit link between human dignity and justice – the affirmation that human dignity is the basis of justice – came three years later in the Preamble to the Universal Declaration of Human Rights, which stated that, "[...] recognition of the inherent dignity and of the equal and inalienable rights of all members of the human family is the foundation of freedom, justice and peace in the world".

"Human dignity" means many things to many people. Some people would prefer to understand it in the elitist, etymological sense of *dignitas*, which bestows special merit, prestige or high rank on a select group, others derive human dignity from particular and mutually exclusive and even hostile religious standpoints according to which humans have dignity because man was made in the image of this or that God, and still others refer to the secular, democratic sense of dignity inherent to all men because man is a rational animal. The briefest glance at the literature[150] gives an idea of the extreme complexity of, and befuddlement in this crucial area of human rights theory. While human rights today are denatured by their separation into different classes in which the most essential right of all – that of material existence – has been demoted to a temporary, highly selective humanitarian concern, human dignity has fared little better because its essential components of freedom and justice have been lost in the mists of sentimentalism, money values, the kitsch of worldly accoutrements, metaphysics and misunderstandings, the latter sometimes deliberate.

The crux of dignity won't be found by dabbling in metaphysical realms and trying to work out which school of philosophy to ground it in, but by recognising that it is inseparable from the notions of justice and freedom. If human dignity is taken as referring to the quality of being worthy of respect, then the focus has to be on the conditions for that respect to be possible: freedom, justice and equality of rights. This then involves bringing the notion of human dignity firmly into the terrain of politics if it is to have any meaningful function as a key concept of human rights.[151]

Human dignity, the grounding principle of human rights, can be tossed into the arena by almost any group for almost any purpose,[152] and this makes some kind of conceptual ordering or priorities all the more urgent, starting out from a conception of universal human rights in terms of what any citizen of any society needs to function as such or, as what he or she is (or can do and be, in the terms of Martha Nussbaum's "capabilities approach" to human rights). The question of how to guarantee the interrelated requirements of freedom, justice and dignity is the next step. What can be salvaged from the notion of "universal" dignity when power and wealth are so concentrated in so few hands that millions of people can be stripped of their human rights? If rights and dignity are not universally distributed, they are at least enshrined in declarations that are declaredly universal, that reach into every part of the globe. This means that they can be claimed universally for, in theory, every single person is entitled to the rights and dignity set out in the Universal Declaration.

Radical

If human rights are to be truly human and truly universal they must be radical. The adjective "radical" can be traced back to the late fourteenth century and its medieval philosophical sense of *radicalis* (of, or having roots), from the Latin *radix*. By the mid-seventeenth century, it had taken on the meaning of "essential" or "going back to the origins" which, by the early nineteenth century, acquired "reformist" hues, via the idea of change flowering from the roots. The second definition given by the

Oxford Dictionary today is, "advocating or based on thorough or complete political or social reform; representing or supporting an *extreme* [emphasis added] or progressive section of a political party". With the stress on "extreme" the word now tends to be given the negative connotations of extremism (fanaticism, violating commonly accepted moral standards and, in today's Manichaean world, frequently linked with Islamic terrorism). The term *radicalisation* is often found in counter-terrorism literature, so heavily loaded with behaviourist spin that the noun *radical* is taken as being synonymous with fanatical and hence *irrational*, and this state of mind can then be detached from the *radically* antihuman conditions a radical might very *rationally* be protesting. The response or aim in this context is to *de-radicalise*. In the case of human rights, part of their de-radicalisation – often into humanitarianism, the consummate power relation – is in their uprooting from early notions of rights with their key associated concepts such as human dignity, citizenship, property, freedom and political economy that are closely related with the basic *radical* deep-rooted assumptions pertaining to the shaping and functioning of coherent social life.

IV

Principles of Natural Truth and Lustre

> Our cause and principles do through their own natural truth
> and lustre get ground in men's understandings; so that where
> there was one, twelve months since that owned our
> principles, we believe there are now hundreds: so that though
> we fail, our truths prosper. And posterity we doubt not shall
> reap the benefits of our endeavours whatever shall become of
> us.[153]

When "human rights" are not being used instrumentally, as for
example in western foreign policy towards China, or in some
attempts to explain why the United States invaded Iraq in 2003,
they are dismissed as a utopian dream, in particular economic
and social rights. Rights aren't utopian. Literally meaning
"nowhere" (from the Greek *ou* + *topos*; "not" + "place"), this
word, coined by Thomas More as the title of his book of 1516
describing an imaginary island governed by perfect social,
political and legal systems, had come to mean "any perfect
place" by the early 1700s. A perfect place would have to be
changeless. Human rights are about the ever-shifting here-and-
now of any time, of real places in a very long struggle for social
justice. If one were to offer a charitable interpretation of this
misuse of the word "utopian", and since the concepts are turned
upside down anyway, it might be couched in terms of Freud's
concept of projection: perhaps the poetry, the "natural truth and
lustre" of these ancient claims, often formulated in really
beautiful language by relatively unlettered people, gives a
glimpse of another kind of place that unbearably shows up the
fact that it is the neoliberal world that is *no place* for humans.

Modern human rights language is grounded in a secular

liberalism that upholds human rights independently of the religious sphere. Many academics argue that the present-day notion of equal and inalienable rights held by any human being can't be found in any western or non-western society before the seventeenth century[154] and that, prior to this, the notion of human dignity functioned in the vertical sense, as a principle of hierarchy.

The oldest, most essential ideas that are the basis of human rights today were not known as "human rights" until much later. They are related with basic, *common*sense[155] notions of fairness or justice, what is right and what is wrong, and a person's sense of his or her own dignity and what, then, should be the proper, *right*, treatment he or she expects on that basis. These ideas are much more closely entwined with the original meanings of the basic human rights words than are liberal "human rights" uses. The memory of past abused rights lays the foundations for the future of human rights, thus linking past and future. Without history and memory, human rights are watered down by legal abstractions, buzzword platitudes and political abuse, aided by the media which intersperses images (sometimes hard to distinguish from those of a computer game, or an action film starring some hunky actor) of real human rights dramas with celebrity antics, "reality" shows and dog food ads. The notion of *universal* human rights remains safely abstract when one only fleetingly sees the horrors of human rights abuse in the comfort of one's living room. Yet there is promise, too, in the right of everybody to know that everybody should enjoy human rights in the same measure, the right of feeling that everybody could belong to a coherent world and not one threateningly fractured between the haves and the have-nots.

The antiquity of notions of justice – and hence rights, human rights – in the public sphere, based on *righteousness* in particular, is evident in the set of laws that Hammurabi, King of Babylon from 1792 – 1750 BCE had inscribed on large stone tablets. In the

Epilogue, he specifically gives an account of his goal of justice and righteous law for the protection of citizens (while discounting the rights of slaves, as Thomas Jefferson was also to do some 3,500 years later when he declared "all men are created equal" in the American Declaration of Independence):

> LAWS of justice which Hammurabi, the wise king, established. A righteous law, and pious statute did he teach the land. Hammurabi, the protecting king am I. I have not withdrawn myself from the men, whom Bel gave to me, the rule over whom Marduk gave to me, I was not negligent, but I made them a peaceful abiding-place. [...] I am the salvation-bearing shepherd, whose staff is straight, the good shadow that is spread over my city; [...] That the strong might not injure the weak, in order to protect the widows and orphans, I have in Babylon the city where Anu and Bel raise high their head, in E-Sagil, the Temple, whose foundations stand firm as heaven and earth, in order to bespeak justice in the land, to settle all disputes, and heal all injuries, set up these my precious words, written upon my memorial stone, before the image of me, as king of righteousness.[156]

In the secular tradition, the search for justice and the outcry against abuse of power is as old as human society and a person who wants justice and who feels that his or her dignity has been offended by some abuse of power has an innate sense of rights that should not be violated by another person. It may have taken a long time to achieve succinct high-level formulation of the revolutionary claims for liberty, equality and fraternity as the inextricably united rights and duties of citizens but the basic concepts were always present among ordinary people. If the Hammurabi Code was concerned with certain liberties and the integrity, accountability and transparency of the legal system, Plato (427/428 – 348/347 BCE) sought eternal notions of truth or forms that represent universals, while Aristotle's *Politics* (350 BCE) showed how ideas of justice, virtue and rights change in accordance with different kinds of constitutions and circumstances, and Epictetus of Hierapolis (135 – 55 BCE) spoke of liberty and "universal brotherhood", ideals shaped by his experience of having been a slave. Epicurus (341 – 270 BCE) contemplated the question of private right, teaching that the state should be formed by a contract concluded between free and equal individuals (excluding slaves), the *syntheke* whose basic principle was the will not to harm each other and whose goal was the useful civic life of each participant in society and the serene coexistence of each with every other. Since the covenant is among equals, subjugation has to be absent among those who are fortunate enough to be free and equal and, given that this presupposes an equality of interests, then an equality of rights among individuals has to be assumed. Greek tragedy, too, made its contribution by showing the deep connections between memory, justice and what is right. Without this historical basis of notions of right, there would be no rights.

The celebrity historian Niall Ferguson peddles the message of *Civilization: The West and the Rest* (yes, he actually gave this title to one of his books), touting a WASP timeline as if "civilisation" were an exclusively western product and Enlightenment notions of human decency were entirely absent among the "Rest". He is far from alone in his western values crusade or as a "fully paid-up member of the neoimperialist gang", as he likes to describe himself, and factual wrongness is no problem for the gang. However, the reality is otherwise. The "Rest" have a great deal to teach the West about human rights values.[157] In the East, Confucius called upon rulers to give an example to the people by showing respect, tolerance and generosity towards others, while his anti-authoritarian critic Zhuang Zi celebrated the human dignity of society's outcasts in a marvellous defence of justice and freedom that is as vibrant and eloquent as any text ever written on the subject. In India, the *Arthashastra* (c. 300 BCE) of the thinker Kautilya (or Chanakaya) called for a transparent judiciary and legal system and would seem to have influenced Asoka (300 – 232 BCE), after his violent beginnings, to practise humane treatment and magnanimity towards all his subjects.

Around the world, people with oral traditions teach communal human rights values in their stories, the basis of their law. Very often, a slow or physically weak animal, like the trickster Tortoise or Anancy the Spider, are given special powers to outsmart bigger, more powerful and greedy animals as they convey the values they wish to teach. These values aren't called "human rights" but they are all about human justice, freedom and dignity. A short "Dream Time" story (about a man, woman, child, or a moth, snake, or platypus, et cetera) of any of the Australian Aboriginal groups can contain up to twenty lessons in respect for one's fellows, animals and surroundings while, for example, an Igbo folktale condensed into Ikemefuna's song in Chinua Achebe's *Things Fall Apart*, shows how values and laws are transmitted in oral traditions and not even kings are exempt. The song goes: *"Eze elina, elina! / Sala / Eze ilikwa ya / Ikwaba akwa oligholi / Ebe Danda nechi eze / Ebe Uzuzu nete egwu / Sala"*. An arrogant king wants to break a taboo and eat the first yams of the crop, usually reserved for the gods. The song warns him not to commit the offence which will bring catastrophe on his people. If he does, he will weep for his crime and pay the price of death, denied proper burial rites and reunion with his ancestors, cast out from the memory of the living community for generations to come and claimed only by the white ant and dust dancing to the drums. Through the law expressed in song, the community tries to keep the king in check to prevent any excess that will harm its members.

The oldest precedents of universal human rights, whatever the setting and terms in which they are expressed, are linked with a more or less universal and constant sense of natural justice, or natural right, rather than with formal legal systems that vary from society to society and from time to time. They posit inherent moral standards that are independent of and above the positivity of existing conditions, thereby providing a normative basis for legitimate criticism and for challenging the status quo. These normative principles have been based on models ranging from physical nature, to God, to human nature and reason, while cognitive approaches to these principles also vary greatly. Indeed, the term "natural law" is full of hazards since it can be used for religious purposes, for defending any status quo as "natural", or "an eye for an eye" or *lex talionis* morality, the principle of exact reciprocity that also appears in Hammurabi's code (§230). "Natural law", in this Manifesto, refers simply to historical notions of justice, which is believed to spring *naturally* from the social conditions required in forming a community of people who want to live together in peace and harmony.

In his *Decretum*, compiled in about 1140, the Benedictine monk Gratian quotes the definition of natural law given by Isidore of Seville:

Natural law is the law common to all peoples, in that it is everywhere held by the instinct of nature, not by any enactment: as, for instance, the union of man and woman, the generation and rearing of children, the common possession of all things and the one liberty of all men, the acquisition of those things which are taken from air and sky and sea; also, the restitution of an article given in trust or money loaned, and the repelling of force with force. For this, or whatever is similar to this, is never considered unjust, but natural and equitable.[158]

Subsequent thinkers debated the inconsistency between "common possession" and scripture-blessed private property. If natural law has been a contentious subject throughout the ages, it is interesting in relation with human rights because of the universal character with which it is endowed in being considered by legal thinkers as "the law common to all peoples, in that it is everywhere held by the instinct of nature, not by any enactment". But property is always skulking behind the scenes.

Natural law, in this ambivalent sense, came to be regarded as the basis of the "Fundamental Laws of England" and was an essential element in the development of English common law. In the struggles between Parliament and the monarch, members of Parliament argued that natural law principles had set limits on the power of the monarchy since time immemorial. The English jurist Henry de Bracton (ca. 1210 – 1268) whose work *Legibus et Consuetudinibus Angliae* (Of the Laws and Customs of England) provided an ethical definition of law, has had an abiding influence in British common law. He considered justice to be the "fountainhead" from which "all rights arise".[159] His definition of justice was taken from the twelfth-century Italian jurist Azo of Bologna: "Justice is the constant and unfailing will to give to each his right."

In the history of the struggle for human rights, the most relevant aspect of "natural law" is the idea that justice is not "created" in positive law or in bills of rights but appears in natural processes of resolving conflicts because it is imminent in nature and is therefore of universal application. The content of positive law can't be determined unless it is on the basis of moral principles that are prior to positive law. While, for legal positivism, a law is no less a law for being unjust, for natural law jurisprudence, an unjust law would be a deficient one.

In the seventeenth and eighteenth centuries there was a shift from discussion of law to a focus on the natural rights of the individual, which paved the way for the revolutionary ideals of the French Revolution: liberty, equality and fraternity. Autonomy and enlightenment became "man's release from his self-incurred tutelage",[160] the individual became a *citoyen*, and "inalienable rights" and the normative ideals of a just society now entered the realms of jurisprudence and politics or, in other words, social questions began to gain more ground in questions of political philosophy. Human dignity, as anticipated or formerly latent in natural law, became insurgent.

In practice, the new revolutionary values were soon redefined by counterrevolutionary distortion. Equality, shorn of any notion of economic justice, was restricted to "equality before the [positive] law" or "before God". Freedom, less amenable to mathematical reckoning than Equality, has today run amok in the form of unbridled "freedom", a dangerous freedom because it spurns ethical responsibility, the fraudulent freedom of the profit motive that crushes the freedom of others and, with this debauched freedom and the culture of impunity it nurtures, the other two values can't exist. It has taken the basic idea that everybody has the right to enjoy the material means of existence and the freedom entailed therein to the sordid extreme that some individuals need to own twelve Lear Jets or a twenty-seven-storey family home in downtown Mumbai,[161] financial capital of India and the "global capital of slum dwelling"[162] just because they think they are free to. Such a gap between rich and poor can't be swept under the rug of any formal or juridical claims of equality. Fraternity was eventually subsumed in amorphous mass notions such as the "melting pot", the Fascist "community", the Third Reich *Volk* and, more recently, into the postmodern potpourri of multiculturalism. Instead of a noble and generous brotherhood and sisterhood among men and women, we are left with little more than a negative definition, the beggarly crumb of the fact that, however suggestive the anthropomorphic resemblances, the jackal and the shark are not members of the human family, although it is also possible that some of the planet's wealthiest inhabitants would sooner recognise kinship with a shark than with a bondsman in Bangladesh, a landless peasant in

Paraguay or a child prostitute in Bombay.

Platitudes about freedom abound, however, because of the many spheres in which it is applicable, but more often than not it is an egoistic freedom, shorn of the idea that the limits of my freedom are defined by respect for yours and everybody's, because respect for equality and fraternity are also missing. This juridically protected freedom, wrote Marx and Engels,[163] is "uncurbed movement, no longer bound by a common bond or by man, of the estranged elements of his life, such as property, industry, religion, etc., whereas actually this is his fully developed slavery and inhumanity." Since Roman law was adopted, positive law has been held in a certain degree of popular mistrust because it was so evident that it protected the powerful and imprisoned or hung critics and the weak or, as Anatole France put it, "The law, in its majestic equality, forbids the rich as well as the poor to sleep under bridges, to beg in the streets, and to steal bread."[164] For some "wicked and seditious",[165] and for others a man of commonsense, Thomas Paine, pointed out in *The Rights of Man* that, "a constitution is not an act of a government, but of a people constituting government" and, more to the point when human rights are concerned, the "continual use of the word Constitution in the English Parliament, shows there is none; and that the whole is merely a form of government without a Constitution, and constituting itself with what powers it pleases."[166]

Less protected by the law, in particular with regard to the social and economic rights that are enshrined in the international declarations, are people whose economic life "consists in the consumption of uses rather than the accumulation of money".[167] A seventeenth-century verse sums it up:

The law locks up the man or woman
Who steals the goose from off the common
But leaves the greater villain loose

Who steals the common from off the goose.

The law demands that we atone
When we take things we do not own
But leaves the lords and ladies fine
Who take things that are yours and mine.

[...]

The law locks up the man or woman
Who steals the goose from off the common
And geese will still a common lack
Till they go and steal it back.

A couple of centuries later, the American historian Howard Zinn
pointed out the same legal inequity, noting that not only do the
laws protect the rights of the propertied at the expense of the
more basic social and economic rights of the propertyless, but he
also showed "how the bill of rights is publicised but not enforced,
how the property laws are enforced but not publicised [... and]
how decorum and propriety fool us and cause us to revere the
law." He took up the note of insurrectionist justice – "... go and
steal it back" – when he "reminded us that often we have to go
outside the legal framework", and that "people in all countries
need the spirit of disobedience to the state [...]."[168] Such *disobedience* in "democratic" countries would entail forcing the state to
abide by its own constitution and the international documents it
has endorsed.

Throughout history, all the old ideas of what is right have
crystallised in rebellions when ordinary people, commoners,
have felt that their rights, their dignity, their freedom, their sense
of justice were abused. Spartacus, the slave who led the Third
Servile War against the Roman Republic (73 – 71 BCE), became an
icon of many other struggles for justice (the German Spartacus

League, for example) and hero of books, films, ballets and musical compositions. Toussaint L'Ouverture, leader of the slave revolt in Haiti (1791 – 1804), was known as the "Black Spartacus". As early as 1381, one of the leaders of the English Peasants' Revolt, the itinerant preacher John Ball, proclaimed in one of his sermons, "From the beginning all men by nature were created alike, and our bondage or servitude came in by the unjust oppression of naughty men. [...] And therefore I exhort you to consider that now the time is come, appointed to us by God, in which ye may (if ye will) cast off the yoke of bondage, and recover liberty." He prefaced these words with the famous question that, once again, brings out age-old ideas of fairness: "When Adam delved and Eve span, who was then the gentleman?"[169] The preacher's incendiary words, urging the peasants who were being deprived of their old use rights to common land to destroy "the great lords of the realm, and after, the judges and lawyers, and questmongers, and all other who have undertaken to be against the commons", were deemed so dangerous, so threatening to the system of usurped privileges and exploitation that a dreadful example had to be made of him and he was subjected to the hideous tortures of being hung, drawn and quartered, after which his head was displayed on a pike on London Bridge.

The revolt's leaders, John Ball, Wat Tyler and Jack Straw all became folk heroes, and there were rebel heroes – known and not so well known – in many other countries too, for example in Russia, where the former galley slave, Ivan Bolotnikov (1565 – 1608), the Cossack leader Stenka Razin (1630 – 1671) and others led insurrections. From the seventeenth to the nineteenth century there were many slave revolts in Brazil, Panama, Jamaica, Suriname, Guyana, Cuba, Curacao, Venezuela, Barbados, the Virgin Islands, the Danish West Indies, in North America, and in the Cape Colony of Africa. The basic yearning for freedom and a life in which all people were treated as human beings and not like chattels and beasts of burden was at the root of all these uprisings wherever they were and whatever course they took.

In the western world, at least, the English commoners and their struggle against the privatisation of land are particularly relevant in the history of human rights struggles, especially with regard to economic and social rights. It is true that the implementation of human rights has fallen far short of the aspirations expressed in the Universal Declaration of Human Rights but, as the Leveller John Lilburne ("Freeborn John") observes, "the natural truth and lustre" of *common*sense ideas of justice, human dignity, freedom, equality – in short human rights – have always shone in the consciousness of "commoners", in the sense both of ordinary people everywhere and those of England who fought against the enclosures that took common land from peasants, thus depriving many of the poorer families of their means of subsistence.

In England, after the Norman Conquest in 1066 at the Battle of Hastings, the Norman and Plantagenet kings brought under the jurisdiction of forest law as much as a quarter of the country's woodlands, thus reserving them for their own pleasure and to take control of the hydrocarbon energy resources. To give just one example of the profligacy of kings, Henry III's Christmas dinner in 1251 featured 430 red deer, 200 fallow deer, 200 roe deer, 1300 hares, 450 rabbits, 2100 partridges, 290 pheasants, 395 swans, 115 cranes, 400 tame pigs, 70 pork brawns, 7000 hens, 120 peafowl, 80 salmon, and lampreys without number all culled from what was once common land.[170]

Prior to this, commoners had enjoyed customary use rights – for subsistence and not bound with the money economy – to common land, which they used for cattle grazing, clearing trees, gardening, letting pigs forage, and collecting wood for fuel, housing, tools and implements. These domestic uses, however, were soon subordinated to the needs of the wider economy of political power. As the kings became more engaged in the crusades, and competition for control of commerce in the Mediterranean grew fiercer, they squeezed peasants and serfs more and more, and their concerted attack on commoning ended up in civil war. In 1203 King John ordered Hugh de Neville, his chief forester to privatise the woods, "to make our profit by selling woods and demising assarts"[171] and thereby to consolidate state power through buying the loyalty of knights, his majesty's men of war, by granting privileges and endowments from forests that had once been everybody's.

The resounding upshot, with the barons now in open rebellion against King John (1166 – 1216), was the Magna Carta, issued in 1215 and addressed to "archbishops, bishops, abbots, earls, barons, justices, foresters, sheriffs, reeves, ministers, and to all bailiffs, and faithful subjects." This was followed in 1217 by the Charter of the Forest, which enshrines the subsistence practice of commoning on lands that were rich in the energy resources of the times. Together, the charters reversed two centuries of royal appropriation of common land and the latter stipulated that, "Every freeman, henceforeth, without Danger, shall make in his own Wood, or in his Land, or in his Water, which he hath within Our Forest; Mills, Spring, Pools, Marsh-Pits, Dikes, or Earable Ground, without inclosing that Earable Ground; so that it be not to the Annoyance of his Neighbours."[172] As for the Magna Carta, while conserving baronial privileges and interests (and indeed it started out as a set of stipulations known as the "Articles of the Barons"), it enshrined four essential principles of modern law, *habeas corpus*, trial by jury, prohibition of torture and due process of law, all of them principles recently violated *inter alia* by the US Patriot Act ("Uniting and Strengthening America by Providing Appropriate Tools Required to Intercept and Obstruct Terrorism" – yet another example of a childish acronym being used to gloss over unscrupulous political designs) signed into law by President

George W. Bush in October 2001, and for which the "democrat" President Barack Obama was "pleased" to sign a four-year extension in May 2011.[173] It's not just human rights declarations that are trampled on, but constitutions too.

This common-law document, and especially the Charter of the Forest – integrated with the Magna Carta in 1297 under the title (first in Latin) of "The Great Charter of the Liberties of England, and of the Liberties of the Forest", a document that is still on the statute books of England and Wales – upheld commoning against enclosures or, in modern terms, common rights against private property. In this sense, it is very suggestive as a moral and legal basis for human rights, since it defended in the clearest of terms the human right on which all others rest, the right to the means of existence. However, common land was soon seen as being too valuable to be left as sustenance for the common people and, Magna Carta or not, it was taken away. This is the long-ago precedent for the world-wide land grab of present times in which no corner of the world, however remote, is spared.

By the twelfth century, open fields in Britain were being closed into privately owned land, a process that proceeded apace, in particular as the demand for English wool grew in the fifteenth and sixteenth centuries and sheep farming became profitable. In *Utopia*, published in 1516, Thomas More makes a direct link between the rise of private landed property and the rise of crime, especially theft, in a process where sheep become devourers of men and a society based on avarice will "first make thieves and then punish them".

> But I do not think that this necessity of stealing arises only from hence, there is another cause of it, more peculiar to England. 'What is that?' said the cardinal: 'The increase of pasture', said I, 'by which your sheep, which are naturally mild, and easily kept in order, may be said to devour men and unpeople, not only villages, but towns; for wherever it is

found that the sheep of any soil yield a softer and richer wool than ordinary, there the nobility and gentry, and even those holy men the abbots are not contented with the old rents which their farms yielded, nor thinking it enough that they, living at their ease, do no good to the public, resolve to do it hurt instead of good. They stop the course of agriculture, destroying houses and towns, reserving only the churches, and enclose grounds that they may lodge their sheep in them.[174]

The enclosures created thieves at both ends of the social scale but they were only punished at one end. The poor stole to eat and, aided and abetted by lawyers, the land-grabbers stole big-time and became well-to-do gentry as George Orwell describes:

They simply seized it by force, afterwards hiring lawyers to provide them with title-deeds. In the case of the enclosure of the common lands, which was going on from about 1600 to 1850, the land-grabbers did not even have the excuse of being foreign conquerors; they were quite frankly taking the heritage of their own countrymen, upon no sort of pretext except that they had the power to do so.[175]

By 1607, there were food riots in Northamptonshire, which soon spread to other industrial localities of the Midlands. Often led by women, the hungry rioters, many of whom were massacred and hanged, were called "diggers" because of their activities in attacking the enclosure hedges with their spades. By 1649, led by Gerrard Winstanley, they had become known as the "True Levellers", and took as their guide a passage from the Acts of the Apostles (4:32), which states, "The group of believers was one in mind and heart. No one said that any of his belongings was his own, but they all shared with one another everything they had." The idea of "levelling" property by digging up and flattening hedges in order to reform the social order was later explained in the *The True Levellers Standard Advanced* (1649) authored by Gerrard Winstanley and the Diggers:[176]

> The work we are going about is this, To dig up *Georges Hill* and the waste Ground thereabouts, and to Sow Corn, and to eat our bread together by the sweat of our brows. And the First Reason is this, That we may work in righteousness, and lay the Foundation of making the Earth a Common Treasury for All, both Rich and Poor, That every one that is born in the Land, may be fed by the Earth his Mother that brought him forth, according to the Reason that rules in the Creation. Not Inclosing any part into any particular hand, but all as one man, working together, and feeding together as Sons of one Father, members of one Family; not one Lording over another, but all looking upon each other, as equals in the Creation; [...]

The Levellers, rural people in the main, literally constituted a grass-*and*-roots movement and a very large one at that. It was nationwide by the years between the First (1642 – 1646) and Second (1648 and 1649) English Civil Wars. Their sense of justice was acute and coherent. On 11 September 1648, they submitted a "Large Petition"[177] to Parliament, signed by some 40,000 people who saw right in the principle formulated by Richard Overton, that "all men are equally and alike born to the like propriety,[178] liberty and freedome", which succinctly links justice-and-freedom with having access to the means of subsistence and equality in economic and social terms. Their main demands were for popular sovereignty in which "all persons alike [are] liable to every law of the land so all persons even the highest might fear and stand in awe". Then, in what amounts to a people's bill of rights, they claimed freedom of worship and speech, reparation to those – poor people – who had been oppressed by the "intolerable mischiefs" of the powers-that-be, as well as guarantees against arbitrary rule and despotism of kings, judges and their henchmen, in the form of trial by a jury consisting of "twelve sworn men", ordinary people such as cobblers and butchers.

In particular, in their lucid understanding of the economic base of human rights, they demanded the just right of subsistence and, most specifically, that the Government should ensure the material conditions of existence of the "Comunality" by opening up "all late Inclosures of Fens, and other Commons, or have enclosed them only or chiefly to the benefit of the poor", warning that their hunger would bring down the great houses, while Gerrard Winstanley called upon the natural principle that "there is no reason that some should have so much and others so little". Their petition for freedom from fear was also inseparable from the political economy and law of the day. Commoners were criminalised and persecuted simply for trying to subsist. The Leveller newspaper *The Moderate* stated on August 7, 1649 that, "We find some of these felons to be very civil men, and say, that if they could have had any reasonable subsistence by friends, or otherwise, they should never have taken such necessitous courses for support of their wives and families". The wealthy Leveller Laurence Clarkson pointed out that the original crime was in the form of private property: "if the creature had brought this world into no propriety, as Mine and Thine, there had been no such title as theft, cheat, or a lie". And this was no local affair but concerned the "Community of Mankind" and the "Community of the Earth". They were talking about basic universal human rights and, as Parliament sought to pass an Act of Oblivion (yes, really!) against the Levellers, they held their ground, demanding "a most honourable Act of perpetual rememberance, to be as a pattern of publik vertue, fidelity, & resolution to all posterity".

The claims of the Levellers were not isolated. They linked up, in a single international system of political economy, with the slave trade and the claims of its victims for their rights. By the eighteenth century, as Peter Linebaugh details in his study of the Magna Carta,[179] "the struggle to preserve commoning in England intersected with trans-Atlantic slavery", not least because timber from the forests was needed to construct the vessels that were plying the routes of the slave and global commodity trades, and the men-of-war that protected them. The connection was enacted on symbolic ground as well. In 1722, white men blackened their faces to claim the rights of commoners, thus going down in history as the "Waltham Blacks". They are graphically described as "a Sooty Tribe [...], some in Coats made of Deer-Skins, others with Fur Caps [...]. There were likewise at least 300 People assembled to see the *Black Chief* and his *Sham* Negroes."[180]

The "Waltham Blacks" protest began when a Mr. Wingfield thought that the local people were taking their commoners' rights too far and decided to fine some of them as an "example" at a time when the protesting local chronicler, the Vicar of Winkfield noted, "the great inducement of late years to purchasing and building in the Forest has been the relaxation or rather annihilation of the Forest Laws".[181] Until then, the commons had furnished subsistence and even medicines for whole families and for the aged, especially at times of unemployment and low wages. The loss to common people, when the great array of offerings from the land were shrunken in their uses to the squandering pleasures and commerce of the rich, is revealed in detail by Linebaugh, who describes how they "gathered fuel, they gleaned after harvest and their children went nutting and berrying, scared crows from the crops, watched the pigs at mast harvest, tended the sheep and gathered wool from the pastures", and cut "quick-growing hazel to make hurdles for folding sheep, to mend hedges and make fences". They made bean-stakes out of the thinner branches and chimney-sweeping brushes by tying holly sprigs to others. "Bulrushes were woven into baskets, mats, hats, chair seats. Rushes were also used for thatch, as netting for wall plaster, good for bedding, and a wrapping for soft cheeses.

Sand was used for scouring and strewing on cottage floors once a week to absorb dirt, dust, grease. Commoners derived menthol from mint, digitalis from foxglove, aspirin from willow bark; buckthorn was a purgative, henbane a narcotic sedative; comfrey good for bruises, celandine said to remove warts, dandelion a diuretic and laxative, feverfew helped those suffering with migraine." The social effects were also very important for, "The allure of commoning arises from the mutuality of shared resources. Everything is used, nothing is wasted. Reciprocity, sense of self, willingness to argue, long memory, collective celebration, and mutual aid are traits of the commoner."[182]

The new proletarian, however, possessed nothing but his or her labour power and was destined to be a human cog in the machine of semi-slavery. The symbolism of the Waltham Blacks, men who dressed in animal skins and blackened their faces so that they looked like slaves, was very powerful and it was reinforced by the ruling classes who saw commoners, once users of rights and now divested of those rights by the handmaiden of appropriation, the Law – and divested of humanity too, for those rights were human rights – as a "sordid race", "arabs and banditti".[183]

Forty "Waltham Blacks" were arrested and held for trial, and seven were hung at Tyburn in December 1723, a punishment legally stipulated in the ferocious "Black Act", which was passed in May that year. Under the Black Act, a variety of poaching-related crimes, including disguising ("blacking") became felonies, which meant that they could potentially be punished with the death penalty. If the Black Act was first aimed at poachers it soon came to be used to crack down on the lower classes in general and to discourage all kinds of protesters. Not long after John Locke was writing about natural law and rights, William Blackstone (1723 – 1780) of Oxford University, the founder of law as an academic discipline, took the word "common" and turned it on its head, now defining private property as "that sole and despotic common which one man claims and exercises over the external things of the world, in total exclusion of the right of any other individual in the universe".[184] The struggle of the commoners for their rights against the enclosures is, with Blackstone's tampering with the word, turned into the noble struggle of rule of law against the terrorism of "arabs" – sound familiar? – and "rough and savage" men. Positive law prevailed over common law, not without also offering the moral of the tale, as spelt out in one document describing the arraignment and hanging of the Waltham Blacks leaders Richard Parvin, Edward Elliot, Robert Kingshell, Henry Marshall, Edward Pink, John Pink and James Ansell.[185] It concluded that, "Idleness must have been the great source of their lawless depredations [...] Exclusive of the duties of religion, young persons cannot learn a more important maxim than that in the scripture; 'the hand of the diligent maketh rich.'" It sounds like Gina Rinehart (see pp. 18-19). The laws might be harsh but the unruly commoners, savages and the Blacks, had to learn that, "sons in the lower ranks of life should remember, that when laws are once enacted, THEY MUST BE OBEYED. Safety lies in acquiescence with, not in opposition to, legal institutions."

One person who found no "safety" with legal institutions was a former African slave, Olaudah Equiano, who had been kidnapped from his Igbo village in West Africa and taken to a plantation in the British colony of Virginia. In a book titled *The Interesting Narrative of the Life of Olaudah Equiano, or Gustavus Vassa, the African*[186] he detailed his sufferings, denounced torture and made it very clear that slavery brutalised everybody: slaves, slavers, overseers, plantation owners, their wives and children, and the whole society. He also detailed the horrific episode of 1781 involving the slave ship "Zong" in which 122 sick slaves were thrown overboard so that the owners could claim insurance (£30 a head) in compensation. The captain, Luke Collingwood, attempted to shelter behind the law that placed responsibility on the underwriters when slaves were thrown overboard because a ship was in danger due to insurrection, even though there was no such danger:

> The insurer takes upon him the risk of the loss, capture, and death of slaves, or any other unavoidable accident to them but natural death is always understood to be excepted: by natural death is meant, not only when it happens by disease or sickness, but also when the captive destroys himself through despair, which often happens: but when slaves are killed, or thrown into thrown into the sea in order to quell an insurrection on their part, then the insurers must answer.

Ten other slaves were also to be thrown overboard but they asserted their own autonomy and dignity at the hour of death and "sprang disdainfully from the grasp of their executioners, and leaped into the sea triumphantly embracing death".[187]

The insurance company refused to settle and, in legal terms, it all boiled down to a fraudulent insurance claim. There was no prosecution for murder against the captain and his crew and the Solicitor General for England and Wales, Mr. John Lee, declared that a master could drown slaves without "a surmise of impropriety". He is recorded as saying, "What is this claim that human people have been thrown overboard? This is a case of chattels or goods. Blacks are goods and property [...]".[188]

In 1774, some fifteen years before his book was published, Olaudah Equiano, a black man who was in danger of being forced back into slavery, dared to expose the racist system by demanding a warrant of *habeas corpus* – as stipulated in the Magna Carta – on behalf of another slave, John Annis, in a justice-seeking process that required whitening his own face in order to gain access to Annis' tormentor. This occurred at the time that Granville Sharp (1752 – 1813) demonstrated that the Magna Carta prohibited slavery, just as the abolitionist movement was getting underway. If the commoners had expressed their claims to their rights by becoming "Blacks", the black slaves, apart from such notable exceptions as Olaudah Equiano, never had the option of becoming white, even temporarily. Forcibly removed from their communities they were forced to express their dignity in another way, understanding that the profit motive itself was their key to resistance, a suicidal resort, like Mohamed Bouazizi's. The most common form of resistance was self-destruction, either by rejection of food and medicine or jumping overboard, or by whatever other means that became available. The Kru people of Liberia came to be regarded as almost useless as slaves since they were so proud, so loath to submit to this outrage to their dignity, that they killed themselves at the first opportunity.

Ships had their own laws and captains, seeing their valuable cargo dwindling, resorted to terror. One captain tied up a woman and dropped her into the water on a rope among the sharks that were following the ship. Although she was quickly pulled up, only the upper half of her body remained.[189] The successful slave rebellion on the Spanish vessel "La Amistad" (Friendship (!)) in 1839 was to have major repercussions in the abolitionist movement. The rebellious slaves explained that, "When we found ourselves at last taken away, death was more preferable than life, and a plan was concerted amongst us, that we might burn and blow up the ship, and to perish all together in the flames".[190] The sailors, ocean-going proletarians, also suffered and were frequently tricked into signing contracts by port tavern owners in league with the slavers, who got them drunk and thus indebted, and then offered to "forget" the debt if they signed up with the slave ships. Otherwise, they faced prison. The screw was turned further in many cases because, on release, the only work that remained open to them was the hated slave ship trade.[191]

Three years before the Waltham Blacks were hanged at Tyburn, the crisis of the commons was accompanied by financial crisis that arose from slavery in the form of an enormous bubble that popped. This was the debacle of the South Sea Company which, at the end of the War of Spanish Succession, had won in 1713 through the Treaty of Utrecht, a thirty-year *asiento* ("settlement" or contract) giving it the exclusive right to sell slaves in all the American colonies. In twenty-five years, it purchased 34,000 slaves, of whom some 4,000 died in the Middle Passage. In a pattern that is all too familiar today (complete with government bailouts), insane speculation by the company – for example, in a wheel of perpetual motion, or the transmutation of quicksilver into a "fine metal" and, best of all, "For carrying on an undertaking of great advantage; but nobody to know what it is" (a precursor of "futures" trading) – one of whose founders and also its Governor was the none other than Lord Treasurer Robert Harley, led to the South Sea Bubble in 1720, causing financial ruin for many people. While this was ostensibly a trading company, Harley had established it with a view to funding government debt incurred during the War. It made extravagant claims, often false, about its stock and its foreign ventures, the famous "Bubbles". In contrast with the popping of today's bubble, the perpetrators had to pay: "One by one the case of every director of the company was taken into consideration. A sum amounting to two millions and fourteen thousand pounds was confiscated from their estates towards repairing the mischief they had done […]."[192]

The economic bubble climate of today has its counterpart in the "intellectual" bubble, a veritable growth industry in which many academics champion neoliberalism or cling to the safe obscurity of jargonistic academic specialisation and airy abstractions of whatever theory is in fashion. Social and economic history, commoning and race are widely ignored and human rights theory tends to be shrunken to either a jaded defence of the status quo or frugally confined to legalistic nuts and bolts issues. To quote Peter Linebaugh again, "the ruling class dumbs us down and the dumbing starts at the top".[193] Claiming human rights, levelling them to achieve a true universal status, might be understood as a latter-day sort of commoning and the hedges, fences and barriers around them could be torn down. People could come to understand that, instead of being yet another instrument of the powerful, they hold out rich social sustenance, like the old forests that provided the right to existence, and community structures based on mutuality and other civic values.

The processes of enclosure (dispossession, land-grabbing) are now global but the effects are much the same as those that the Levellers and Commoners lamented, except in scale and the invisibility of the perpetrators. Theft comes to remote places in "legal" guise and global economic relations in the form of prices, migration and remittances tear apart the social fabric of indigenous communities, "introducing the language of monetary circulation that opposes relations of solidarity and mutual concern and support", as the Mexican economist Alejandro Nadal very well describes.[194] Indicators of economic growth, and in particular GDP, which determine the non-future of indigenous peoples, are contemptuous of traditional economies, especially if the communities concerned are occupying land with resources that can be grabbed, as happens with the Yanomami people of the Amazon (ranching, gold mining); the Adivasi, the "first people" of Bangladesh (deforestation, appropriation of common land and water); the Australian Aborigines (their ancestral mineral-rich land); the Amungme, mountain "descendents of the oldest son of the human race" and the lowland tree-dwelling Kamoro people of West Papua (the biggest open-cut copper mine in the world, property of the world's worst polluter Freeport McMoRan, which has given its name to the Freeport McMoRan Chair of Environmental Policy (sic), at the Tulane University of New Orleans); the Nadleh Whut'en, Nak'azdli, Takla Lake, Saik'uz, and Wet'suwet'en First Nations of Northern Alberta (oil sands); ... and so many, many more indigenous communities who face so many, many more kinds of exploitation and, often, eventual extinction. Community relations are consigned to the slag heap of progress. Yet, for all this and when mainstream academia has been dragooned and beguiled into the neoliberal cause, the commoners' response is the one that is the most suggestive and, once again, part of it is coming from the Arab ("arab") countries.

The new commoners' claims are also being made from Chiapas, where the Zapatistas, in the midst of Mexico's "dirty wars", are calling for the return of the *ejido* or common land, which is enshrined in Article 27 of the Constitution, the legal foundation of the distribution of community-owned lands. This was one of the victories of the Revolution of 1917 and it endured until 1992 when the Salinas Government put paid to the country's old commitment to land reform involving about half of Mexico's farmlands by modifying Article 27 at the insistence of the United States prior to Mexico's joining NAFTA (North American Free Trade Agreement), with which the IMF structural adjustment programmes kicked in (and kicked out). If the law of the state not only fails to protect, but also introduces federal policies that threaten the survival of some 25 million peasant farmers, the Zapatistas return to commoning principles, based on democratic decentralisation of power to the community level, autonomy that requires respect for customs and traditions, transparent government in which "bad government" is rejected (including accepting financial assistance from the State Government), and five rotating Juntas of Good Government, which carry out the functions of local and regional constitutional governments, this entailing economic and legal decisions, education, health care and collective development. They also supply detailed accounts of their finances for public scrutiny. Moreover, an oversight committee acts as a watch dog against abuse of power.

In general, the question of law and its relation with the cause of rights has not figured prominently on the agenda of social revolution. If they are to come together, then fundamental changes will have to occur in the structure of political thought. Ecuador has taken some steps in this direction. In 2008, sixty-five per cent of the population voted in favour of a new *"Buen Vivir"* Constitution that contained nothing less than a rights-based system of environmental protection in which natural law and positive law come together. This "Good Living" (in the sense of *right* (rights) living) invoked in the Constitution was concerned with protecting human beings by protecting the human milieu, giving rights not just philosophical but legal status, in the form of *garantismo* – guaranteeing common rights under the law. Hence a judge in Ecuador has to decide on matters of social and economic rights in court in a way that doesn't happen in other parts of the world. Article 71 of Chapter 7 states:

> Nature or Pachamama [Mother Nature], where life is repro-duced and exists, has the right to exist, persist, maintain and regenerate its vital cycles, structure, functions and its processes in evolution.
>
> Every person, people, community or nationality, will be able to demand the recognitions of rights for nature before the public organisms. The application and interpretation of these rights will follow the related principles established in the Constitution.[195]

Article 59 harks directly back to the Charter of the Forest in stating that "[...] persons, people, communities and nationalities will have the right to benefit from the environment and form natural wealth that will allow wellbeing." Unsurprisingly, this radical pairing of the ancient ideas of commoners and constitu-tional law in a legal enshrinement of basic human rights was mainly ignored by the media or ridiculed if mentioned. The *Los Angeles Times* (2 September 2008) dismissed it as "crazy" and suggested it sounded "like a stunt by the San Francisco City

Council" and, needless to say, the Ecuadorian legal system soon found ways to subvert the constitutional ideal. As early as March 2009, after President Rafael Correa's new Mining Law had found enough loopholes so as not to prohibit mining in zones with endangered species, or the dumping of toxic waste in rivers, indigenous leaders filed a lawsuit before the Constitutional Court, citing the second paragraph of Article 1 in a bid to overturn the new law as unconstitutional.

The history of human rights shows that they have generally arisen from among the dispossessed and the disempowered, only to be mediated and given shape by the privileged classes, either in revulsion for atrocities (as with slavery) or, more usually, as a damage management strategy that keeps basic structures in place while offering some kind of sop that will eventually be undermined by the selfsame basic structures. Thomas Rainsborough (1610 – 1648), one of the Leveller leaders, along with John Lilburne, made no bones about the relationship between democracy and property: "Either poverty must use the power of democracy to destroy the power of property, or property in fear of poverty will destroy democracy".[196] His contemporary Lilburne was a leveller of rights and championed what he called "freeborn rights", rights that every human being is born with, as opposed to those bestowed by government and laws. His early distinction between natural and institutional rights is important because the location of human rights in declarations without mechanisms for their guarantee in legal systems has made human rights visible enough to be invoked for all sorts of purposes but not viable. Then the "commoner's", everybody's commonsense (commoner's sense) grasp of principles of justice are scoffed at by the likes of Jeane Kirkpatrick. If "... property in fear of poverty will destroy democracy", it is because the propertied, too, are aware of the moral power of claims that can be made on the basis of age-old, natural commoner's laws and react with commensurate violence when it comes to protecting their possessions and privileges.

In the last ten years new kinds of political parties and civil society movements have begun to appear in Latin America, opening up innovative forms of citizen participation in the political process and opposing neoliberal rapacity. The recent wave of democratic rebellion in the countries of North Africa and the Middle East has ushered in a different kind of politics. This will have high and low points but it won't go away as it is grounded in a very long history. At a crucial point of the Egyptian uprising in the early months of 2011, the internet activist Wael Ghonim said, "We knew we would win when people began to break through the psychological barrier, when they decided that it was better to die for a cause than to live without dignity ... We're stronger than those [Mubarak's] guys because they fear for their lives while we're ready to give ours."[197] Wael Ghonim is talking about the core value of human dignity. He is challenging not just the powers-that-be in Egypt but in the world because he understands that all tyrants, thieves and despoilers of human dignity live in fear of their lives, like the drug barons described by Don Winslow. In their stead he is demanding citizen participation. A citizen is someone with legally-recognised rights and duties. In order to exercise those rights and perform those duties, he or she must enjoy the means to be a civilised person, a good citizen, and this entails re-establishing the ancient links between liberty, equality and fraternity because the basic condition for being a good citizen is receiving from and bestowing respect on others.

The mirror held up by the young protestors today reflects a neoliberal system in disrepute. To paraphrase another Manifesto, the system produces its own grave-diggers.[198] Everybody can see the connection between the liberalisation – "freeing" – of capital flows and the present global downturn which is displacing and dispossessing millions of agricultural producers and small-scale local entrepreneurs. Economists and technocrats, more or less committed servants of the political and economic order that delivers their sinecures, have certainly not come up with an alternative, even as the system is collapsing around their ears. Mohamed Bouazizi has shown the way by throwing his civilised accusation in the face of barbarians.

"The past is the present, isn't it? It's the future too. We all try to lie out of that but life won't let us."[199] The commoners' struggles, their modern-day versions in Chiapas and Ecuador, and an age-old legitimacy in ordinary people's sense of justice, can be the basis of a concerted claim to the commonweal of universal human rights. This is the ground from which Mohamed Bouazizi claimed his human rights, as have so many other people across the world, the same common ground from which the oppressed, throughout history and everywhere, have asserted their dignity, calling for the rights without which they – we – can't be full members of human society.

V

A Human Rights Republic: The Right and Duty of Revolution

"Philosophers have hitherto only interpreted the world in various ways; the point is to change it."[200]

Talking about the "global one per cent", the richest people on earth, and the rest of us, the 99 per cent, is a slogan-form way of describing the enormous gap in wealth and privilege of very few people compared with the poverty of very many, but it doesn't address a *system* that is geared to protecting the structure of concentrated wealth, a legally fortified and militarily ironclad system in which, willy-nilly, we all participate and even sustain to a greater or lesser extent. The NATO countries in which many of us pay taxes, account for 85% of the world's "defence" outlay, and the United States' military spending is higher than that of the rest of the world combined. There has been a clear shift from the welfare state to the surveillance state. This entails greatly expanded public and private security forces, increasingly curtailed public use of public space, drone killings and other extrajudicial assassinations, rising incarceration rates – more than six million people are under "correctional supervision" in the United States and, by 2008, more than one in every hundred people (one in every 36 Hispanic adults and one in every fifteen Afro-American adults) was behind bars[201] – and new forms of social exclusion that are now appearing in legal codes. In 1831, after touring American prisons, Alexis de Tocqueville wrote in his *Democracy in America* that, "In no country is criminal justice administered with more mildness than in the United States". Now, with five per cent of the world's population, the United States accounts for more than a quarter of its prison population and, if "mildness" ever was a feature of the country's penitentiaries, it is certainly a thing of the past. According to the Justice Department, in 2008 "more than 216,600 people were sexually abused in prisons and jails and, in the case of at least 17,100 of them, in juvenile detention. Overall, that's almost six hundred people a day – twenty-five an hour."[202] In brief, the increased military, police and legal repression being applied around the world to deter any states, social movements or individuals that might try to resist the global dominance of the super-rich takes us straight back to Thomas Rainsborough's warning that "property in fear of poverty will destroy democracy". As we bear helpless witness to a world that is becoming more inhuman every minute, the question – do we want a human world? – is ever more urgent. If we want a human world it must be based on human rights.

The basic principle of commoning "all for one and one for all" – or, as Marx and Engels put it, "the free development of each is the condition for the free development of all"[203] – is a notion that many people scoff at or, if they recognise it at all, they swat at it like some pesky red fly but, at times of upheaval, this spirit appears again and again: in Tahrir Square in Cairo, in the other insurgent cities of the Arab world, in the cities of Greece and, more recently, in the United States and in squares all over Spain with the revolt of the *indignados* who have defied government bans on their assemblies. In *The Rights of Man* Thomas Paine observes that in the American Revolution (1775 – 1783), "there were no established forms of government. [...] Yet during this interval, order and harmony were preserved as inviolate as in any country in Europe. [...] The instant formal government is abolished, society begins to act. A general association takes place, and common interest produces common security."

The commoners' spirit still surges today at times of disaster when, as everyday concerns vanish, people find common cause and there are glimpses of another kind of society as they rally to help each other and take social and political initiative. The potential of this "common interest" can be gauged from the official response. The press and the authorities tend to ignore the resilience and "general association" of people affected by a disaster, attempting to disempower them by stereotyping them as frightened, disoriented paralysed victims, or scaremongering with opinions that "civilisation" is very fragile, when the *civil* part of civilisation is actually flourishing in adversity. They are portrayed as "panic-stricken" beasts who, deprived of their usual possibilities of consumption, "stampede" and "loot" (a word more related with the strong than the weak since it originally referred to the act of plundering and spoils of war) when in fact they are collecting food, water and other goods for their own and others' survival. The reality is different, as Rebecca Solnit argues when she discusses media coverage of the Haiti earthquake in 2010:[204] "... the survivors are almost invariably more altruistic and less attached to their own property, less concerned with the long-term questions of acquisition, status, wealth, and security, than just about anyone not in such situations imagines possible." Bereft of credit cards, shops and with a paralysed market, people start shaping another sort of society. Journalists, still equipped with their credit cards, computers, cell phones, a plane ticket out and all the trappings of this other world, see crime instead of emergency requisitioning.

The authorities don't take long to see the threat to the corner-stone of their power. Private property quickly takes precedence over human life. After the earthquake of 18 April 1906 that devastated San Francisco, armed police, patrolmen and students roamed the streets with orders to shoot "looters" on sight. Citizens are thrust back into the pigeonhole of consumers but in a negative way because, now they have lost the means to consume, they are redundant, potential "arabs and banditti", a threat. After the catastrophe of Hurricane Katrina in August 2005, people were imprisoned in the New Orleans Superdrome and the

Convention Center. Armed men at Gretna Bridge, one possible escape route, were turning refugees back by firing over their heads. Shepard Smith, for Fox News, usually the voice of power, was shocked enough to depart from the usual line, reporting instead, "They got locked in there. And anyone who walks up out of that city now is turned around. You are not allowed to go to Gretna, Louisiana, from New Orleans, Louisiana. Over there, there's hope. Over there, there's electricity. Over there, there is food and water. But you cannot go from here to there. The government will not allow you to do it. It's a fact."[205] In an interview with UPI, Arthur Lawson, the police chief of the predominantly white, middle-class Gretna, didn't mince his words when he explained why the bridge had been shut, "If we had opened the bridge, our city would have looked like New Orleans does now: looted, burned and pillaged."[206] Then again, we have the example of Jabbar Gibson, a young man with a petty criminal record who took over a school bus and evacuated about seventy of his New Orleans neighbours to Houston. For the authorities this only compounded his previous felonies because he was said to have illegally appropriated a vehicle of over 26,000 pounds and driven it without the requisite class A, B, or C Louisiana license. The power-market-catastrophe relationship was crudely highlighted by President George W. Bush when, in his Address to the Nation on 20 September 2001, just nine days after the 9/11 attacks, he exhorted the American people, to keep spending: "Fly and enjoy America's great destination spots. Get down to Disney World in Florida. Take your families and enjoy life, *the way we want it to be enjoyed.*"[207]

The basic principles of communing, detailed by the historian Peter Linebaugh,[208] can be summarised as follows:

1) *It is best understood as a verb rather than as a pooled resource, as an activity conducted in a unity of labour and natural resources.*

2) *It is something at the historical heart of almost all societies in the world, basic to human life.*

Recent studies might even make one wonder about whether commoning is wired into us. Ostracism or exclusion is one of the most terrible punishments that one person can inflict on another. Brain scans show that such rejection is experienced as physical pain, whether those that reject us are close to us or total strangers, and even if it only entails somebody averting their eyes.[209] We need to feel we are together.

3) *It begins in the family or kinship group, the production and reproduction coming together in the kitchen or hearth, the sharing of tasks between genders and generations, distribution of the product and mutual caring and sustaining of good health.*

In West Papua, land of a slow almost unreported genocide over nearly fifty years,[210] singing together expresses everything the people do in common, with songs for climbing a mountain – certain songs for certain mountains – for tilling the soil, for the sweet potato seed so that it will grow strong and the earth will be happy, for the fireside, for courting, for loss, anger, the people's love of freedom and their right to independence. The songs are the common heritage and wealth of the people. West Papuan highlanders call the soul *etai-eken* (seed of singing).

4) *Commoning is of the past, yet it keeps cropping up again and again, returning in communes and social and political projects.*

One of its modern forms would be in digital commoning, digging out the truth behind the news or levelling access to information, as with Wikileaks. Of course, the perverted traducing of the concept also appears with gated communities or a police chief's protection of the well-off members of his beat against "looters".

5) *It has a deep spiritual sense of agape, or fraternity, as might arise in the sharing of a meal (the word "commons" also meaning dining hall), in breaking bread together.*

Poor families of Eritrea, for example, are exemplary in this sharing and hospitality as they sit on the floor around a circular woven tray of food (*meadi* in Tigrinya, meaning "to be shared" and denoting at once the food, the tray, the people sitting around it and the social process that this entails) to which any comer is welcome. Everybody, down to the smallest child, knows exactly how much to reduce his or her portion to accommodate the guest. The circle (with a meaning dating from 1714 of "group of persons surrounding a centre of interest", with a common interest) appears again in Asmara with children from families without electricity sitting around streetlamps doing their homework, the smaller ones inside, protected and supervised by the bigger ones.[211]

6) *Commons (from* co- *denoting "together" and* mei *meaning "exchange") and capital (from* capitalis *"of the head", hence chief or first; and "capital", as in crime, or in late fourteenth-century English and in Latin, deadly or mortal) are antithetical.*

As the means of production are expropriated, exploitation – the infringement of the basic rights of freedom, equality and fraternity – shows up, yet again, the material basis of human rights. Capital, the head, turns to ideologies of economics and social and "libertarian" theory that are a travesty of liberty to tell us that that "common" (exchanged together) ideas are utopian, a "letter to Santa Claus", or that ethics can only take the form of "lifeboat" (like the slave ship "Zong") ethics where the weak but dangerous people who do not have the means to be consumers (from *consumere*, early fifteenth-century, "one who squanders and wastes" or "takes") have to be thrown overboard or be locked up in "humanitarian" camps. As Linebaugh comments, "They always assume as axiomatic that concept expressive of capital's bid for eternity, the a-historical 'Human Nature'".[212]

7) *Commoning values need to be transmitted, handed down, taught and continually renewed.*

Renewal can happen when people forget about the mores of capital (the invisible head of state) and go back to *common* sense, understanding that if they don't claim their own rights nobody is going to do it for them. Then people's assemblies start appearing, from Brasilia, to Oaxaca, to Detroit, to Wisconsin, to Madrid, to London.

8) *While the idea is universal, commoning activity is local.*

In each place, commoning rests on humanity's shared things like custom (from the Latin *consuetumen,* referring *inter alia* to common usage and familiarity), memory, stories, and the oral transmission of norms and justice. Independently of the apparatus of state, the community-based Gacaca courts in Rwanda, whose judges are called *Inyangamugayo* ("persons of integrity" in the Kinyarwanda language) and are elected from the localities where the accused are alleged to have committed the crime, have quietly brought some measure of justice and recon-ciliation to the stricken country. For Australian Aborigines, the law is in the ground common to the group. They navigate the land by singing the landscape, constantly reviving the footprints of their ancestors in its features, seeking permission from other groups to cross their territory in a language of melodic contours and rhythms that overcomes differences in spoken tongues, fostering order and harmony between peoples and people and land in a commonly constructed map that offers both ethical and geographic guidance.

9) *"Common" is different from "public".*

"Common" (c. 1300, from Latin *communis*) originally meant general, free, shared and open to all, not pretentious, while "public" is related with the more neutral *populus,* or people. After 1826 its meaning warped into publicity, the tool of capital, fosterer of individual indulgence and egotism.

10) *The commons "has always been an element in human production".*[213]

People have to work together somehow and the seed of the commons is always there, waiting to flower. Even in the poorest parts of newly industrial London, workers established reading rooms and saw reading and study as a social activity based on mutual self-help, a commoning of the mind, reading aloud for mutual education, in pubs, on street corners, at Chartist meetings and Methodist circles. In workshops, one labourer commonly read aloud while the others shared his work. About half of all working-class people between 1870 and 1918 practised reading aloud in their homes as they shared their scant resources in the interests of improving the common lot.[214] Commoning requires people to work together, whether on the factory floor, in reading groups or, nowadays, when the latent seed springs into life in the streets and squares of the planet. Rights and duties go together. Indeed, although the authorities constantly flout it, the First Amendment to the United States Constitution equates the rights of speech, assembly and that of petitioning the state to meet its obligations to citizens: "Congress shall make no law respecting an establishment of religion, or prohibiting the free exercise thereof; or abridging the freedom of speech, or of the press; or the right of the people peaceably to assemble, and to petition the Government for a redress of grievances."[215] This "intercourse of the commons"[216] is a necessary component of human thought.

11) *The powers-that-be must learn that forgetting or suppressing the past is no escape from it.*

The commoners' old ideals appear now in human rights claims. This Manifesto is about their principles, the ones that should apply to universal human rights: a pooled (universal) resource; well-founded historically; inseparable from the conditions of production and reproduction; levelling differences of equality and access to the universal common wealth of rights; fraternal, respectful towards others in the duties they entail; sharing; antithetical to the values of capital, consumption and neoliberal notions of entitlement and impunity; requiring constant perusal and renewal, respectful of others; and needing to be understood as an element of political economy.

Human rights commoning, which is to say truly universal human rights would then have to be part of some kind of human rights republic. Would this, too, be a "nursery tale"? A "utopia"? Or would it be a radical new way of thinking about a world that seems, on almost every front, to be bankrupt and corrupt, ruptured? The powers-that-be typically defend the *status quo*, however cracked it is. But what the law might define as "reasonable" in one "current situation" – for example when women were too "irrational" to vote – is idiotically unreasonable in another. The *status quo* itself is always changing, not least because of the demands of The Market. Normative changes favouring justice, freedom, equality, fraternity, democracy and human rights come from social movements, an awakening of consciousness – *Indignez-vous*, as the old resistance fighter Stéphane Hessel urged – a *re*surgence of age-old claims appearing now as *in*surgence. This alone may not solve the problems but it does take them from the personal to the political sphere, presenting them in a new light and revealing the injustices that lurk behind rhetoric.

The modern human rights movement, embodied above all in the Universal Declaration of Human Rights and the Convention on the Prevention and Punishment of the Crime of Genocide (9 December 1948), was a response to the atrocities and violations of human rights before and during the Second World War, but it was also based on much earlier notions of justice, which were seen as a counterbalance against legal positivism, which claims that there is no necessary connection between the validity conditions of law and ethics or morality. Mainly exhortative, human rights declarations and conventions have come to shape a substantial normative reference for movements that are starting to give a real international dimension to human rights. The post-war national liberation movements, the internal debilitation of the Soviet Union (which in 1975 signed the Helsinki Accords, the final act of the Conference on Security and Cooperation in Europe entailing acceptance of some human rights demands) and local democracy movements that sprang up in different parts of

Latin America in the 1970s and 1980s have made their mark on the human rights situation in a wide variety of places. Now, with all kinds of human rights activists speaking out from everywhere, big cities and tiny communities in once-unnoticed corners of the world, human rights are becoming rather more than an expression of liberal "freedoms" but have taken up the banner of justice and are becoming a new commoners' power in world politics.

This international dimension took a discouraging turn after 1989 when human rights were increasingly used selectively to justify sanctions, military invasions and so-called "humanitarian" interventions under cover of international law and the R2P (responsibility – understood as "right" when deemed necessary – to protect), most notably in the cases of Bosnia, Afghanistan and Iraq. And what about the people of West Papua? Do they have no right to be protected? It would seem that the "responsibility" to "protect" and the right to be protected are very different matters. The former is highly selective even while the latter is supposedly universal, at least for children, as declared in the Convention on the Rights of the Child (1990).[217] No concerted international attempt has ever been made to stop the ongoing Indonesian genocide in West Papua and, it was only in 1999, twenty-four years after the Indonesian invasion and genocidal occupation of East Timor, which took the lives of up to 200,000 people (a third of the population at the time of invasion), that international pressure was exerted on Indonesia to permit a referendum on self-determination. Even so, the international organisms were not prepared for the killings, massive displacement of the population and the scorched earth and blanket-destruction policies that followed. Human rights movements have started heading in a new direction, now focusing on the economic, social and civil rights of indigenous populations, especially in Latin America, Australia and Canada (from whence the new Idle No More movement of the First

Nations people is presently spreading fast around the world), even as the nation state has ceased to be the main locus of human rights with the issuing of new United Nations conventions, the establishment of the European Court of Human Rights and the International Criminal Court, not to mention international migratory movements and the economic and financial globalisation which affects us all.

This is a two-edged sword. Surely, if there is a R2P, however scantily formulated it is – as if to cover up the fact that the great powers are the ones that wield this highly partial "responsibility" (to protect what?) as a right without duty – then there must also exist a right to *be protected* from the depredations of the whole global system, a right whose name should be pronounced loud and clear and not hiding behind some silly acronym, so beloved by the powers-that-be, as if common folk are so easily duped. While self-interested military interventions of sovereign states have been dressed up as international human rights concerns, demands for universal rights are growing louder every day on international networks and there is new awareness of their roots in the eternal human struggle for justice. Indigenous peoples are starting to find a voice, to organise and fight for their rights, and they have a legal instrument to appeal to, the United Nations Declaration on the Rights of Indigenous Peoples (September 2007), which recognises the rights of some 400 million people, including economic rights and that of redress, as appears in Article 20:

Article 20:
1. Indigenous peoples have the right to maintain and develop their political, economic and social systems or institutions, to be secure in the enjoyment of their own means of subsistence and development, and to engage freely in all their traditional and other economic activities.
2. Indigenous peoples deprived of their means of subsistence

and development are entitled to just and fair redress.[218]

Where are mechanisms to ensure that the holders of these promised rights know about them, can act on them and that they will be implemented and guaranteed by the international and national institutions? The historical links between colonialism, racism, exploitation, dispossession, poverty, immigration and huge gaps of wealth and power can no longer be hidden. One significant aspect of present claims for human rights is that this is a struggle of populations, commoners, against the powers-that-be, whatever form it takes. Liberal jurisprudence, bound by its history of property rights and individualism, and with scant sense of history, cannot properly interpret these developments. Recent people's movements show that human rights must be linked with social interests and social conflicts in order to under-stand how these developments have come about, and how they should be answered in human rights terms with some kind of international charter equipped with institutional mechanisms to guarantee human rights as the basis of something like a global human rights republic.

If mechanisms for the guarantee of human rights are missing in the charters existing to date, there are also some other inter-esting omissions that might work in favour of the dispossessed. The International Covenant on Civil and Political Rights (1976)[219] doesn't enshrine the right to property as such, while the United Nations Human Rights Committee only deals with individual property rights to the extent that they entail discrimination or inequality before the law. Although the matter isn't entirely clear, in the International Covenant on Economic, Social and Cultural Rights (1976)[220] property rights would seem to be subservient to other basic rights such as food and shelter. In other words, in international jurisprudence, if not in national legal systems, property rights can be interpreted as being subordinate to basic human economic and social rights. Unbridled property rights are wreaking havoc everywhere but they are also looking more and more like a relic of feudal times, sustained nowadays by a celebrity culture that would probably shock Adam Smith, who observed more than 250 years ago that, "The disposition to admire, and almost to worship, the rich and the powerful and ... neglect persons of poor and mean condition [...] is the great and most universal cause of the corruption of our moral sentiments."[221] Real dignity, the bedrock of human rights, which has a great deal to do with moral sentiments, to the extent that one's human dignity should always be understood and valued in relationship with the human dignity of everyone else, is the opposite of celebrity. You can have it but it's not for sale, and it tends not to inhabit palaces and mansions. However, human dignity, which requires at least the basic means of subsistence, is denied to millions of "persons of poor and mean condition" by poverty that is to a great extent the counterpart of the insatiable thirst for celebrity of "the rich and powerful".

Poverty is usually presented as a technical problem of lack of material resources or of access to them without reference to the causes of this situation. Moreover, this "morally unacceptable want",[222] or injustice, is a problem of the individual's exercise of his or her capabilities as a member of society. Freedom is the basis of morality – which pertains essentially to human dignity – because a critical aspect of freedom derives from the temporal and especially the forward-looking aspect of the self. Since the rational human, concerned with more than the immediate satisfaction of animal needs, freely projects into the future, he or she is able to experience the consequences of present actions. This is a moral action: the present self is responsible for the condition of the future self. In a situation of persistent extreme poverty, without freedom, the human is reduced to the barest animal expression of the temporal self and its immediate needs, like the Ik, and the forward-looking – moral, and hence social and civic-minded – self is virtually without existence. The issue becomes a very practical one: what does a human being need in order to be free to exercise his or her social capabilities, and how might this be achieved?

The classical republican tradition[223] gives priority to instruments that can guarantee the essential rights deriving from the material independence of individuals, as the basis of their freedom in social life which, left to itself without some kind of institutional intervention, tends to generate all manner of asymmetries of power. This is where political economy comes in, identifying the social forces at work in the world, understanding social life as a space seething with power relations at all levels, and thus indicating the need to construct an institutional framework with mechanisms that guarantee to prevent the appearance of great asymmetries of power that lead to relations of domination among individuals or, in other words, institutional means that can forestall the historical resorts to ascendancy that sustain these social relations.

The basic principle that can be drawn from classical republicanism in this regard is that a person can't be free without a guaranteed material existence because, when anybody is dependent on others for sustenance, he or she has to obtain their permission to live, day after day. Poverty jeopardises the possibility of consuming and, in particular, producing certain goods that enable real citizenship and life in the community. Then the undermining of the person's civic dignity and certain types of social pathology only compound the problem of exclusion and deprivation, making it increasingly difficult to claim his or her rights. Through dependence, the person is forced into a non-person's unfree status of *alieni iuris*, subject to an alien regime. About half the world is in that situation today.

Democratic republicanism holds that the political community must ensure that the material existence of *all* citizens is politically guaranteed. It must accordingly pledge to *all* citizens a certain agreed-upon set of material resources that would bestow on them conditions of material and civic independence and freedom from arbitrary interference that are comparable to those enjoyed by the propertied members of society. However, the institutions of contemporary societies are based on property rights, whatever the form of property, on the basis of which rich (independent people) and poor (dependent people) are drastically segregated because the rich are free to enjoy much more than their share of resources while the poorer members of the community, with very few resources, typically have to sell their labour five or more days a week to the owners of these material resources in order to subsist. If they have work, they are wage labourers, subject to the will of others and, if they don't have work, they are even more excluded.

Nowadays, individuals or groups of individuals who wield great economic power, for example exceedingly rich people or transnational corporations, gain sweeping control over the material resources of entire populations. Through their power in the media they can dictate tastes and then hold out the dubious privilege of buying the many stupid, uncomfortable and even dangerous products they have imposed (why on earth would women want to have silicon-"enhanced" breasts, rigid assembly-line botoxed faces, or to shave off their public hair and "vajazzle" their "vajayjays" with Swarovski crystals?) while also preventing vast numbers of people from producing essential goods, food in particular. They therefore interfere arbitrarily in the sets of life-plan opportunities of individual citizens because they can manipulate supply and demand and mould the structure of markets and, accordingly, determine the nature of national economies. They can impose, in productive units – and in parliaments as well – the conditions of work of those who depend on them in order to live. One only needs to look at the role of the rating agencies in influencing the conditions for loans (draconian cuts in public spending, for example) in countries like Greece, Portugal and Spain. In rich and poor countries alike, they can flick the stock exchange wand and dispossess millions of poor people of the means necessary to sustain traditional forms of life and of alternative resources for managing productive realms, and they can sway political decisions and agendas.

In November 2007, the Universal Declaration of Emergent Human Rights was approved at the Universal Forum of Cultures in Monterrey. Article 1.3 reads:

> The right to a basic income or universal citizen's income that guarantees to every human being, independently of age, gender, sexual orientation, civil or employment status, the right to live in material conditions of dignity. To this end, a regular cash payment, financed by tax reforms and covered by the state budget, and sufficient to cover his or her basic needs, is recognised as a right of citizenship of every member-resident of the society, whatever his or her other sources of income may be.[224]

The importance of Article 1.3 of the Monterrey Declaration is that it transforms the usual way of addressing the most basic human right from being something ephemeral and detached from human society into an institutional mechanism specifically designed to guarantee the basic freedom required for the realisation of all other human rights. Instead of speaking vaguely of the "right to subsistence" or of having certain minimal vital needs covered in case of the onset of poverty or some catastrophe, it upholds the clearly designated "right to a basic income or universal citizen's income" as an ongoing guarantee to every single individual of the "right to live in material conditions of dignity". In effect, this means pledging that no individual will be excluded from engaging in social life and exercising his or her rights and duties as a citizen because of acute poverty, thus making democratic participation possible for everyone. It conceives of this right on a universal scale, for rich and poor, developed or developing countries alike.

This basic income[225] could be of enormous importance as an integral part of a package of measures designed to guarantee the material existence of all people and their possibilities of living according to their own life plans by means of "universalising [commoning] property" in this form, which would then universalise the essential condition of truly effective citizenship. The idea of universalising "property" can't be taken too literally but should simply be understood as providing the essential conditions for material, and hence social existence to everyone. A guaranteed basic income, above the poverty line, for everybody, would offer an autonomous base of existence that would be much firmer and infinitely more widespread than that available to a good part of today's citizens, especially in the more vulnerable and most subjugated sectors (wage workers, the poor in general, the socially excluded, the unemployed, women, et cetera).

In both rich and poor countries, the economic independence furnished by a basic income, paid not to households but to individuals, would establish a kind of domestic "counter-power" that could modify relations of domination between the sexes by increasing the bargaining power of women especially those who are dependent on the husband or male head of the family, or those whose earnings are very low in badly paid, part time or discontinuous employment. Farmers in the poor countries and workers in the developed countries are in a precarious situation. In capitalist countries, unemployment is comparable with the landlessness of small farmers in agrarian societies because what brings these two apparently very different economies together is the fact that dispossession in both private and public spheres, of land and of other means of production, is a prominent feature of the capitalist system and, still more acutely since the end of the 1970s, of the neoliberal system which, one way or another and largely negatively, affects everybody. The dispossessed must sell their labour – usually in terribly exploitative conditions – to the person who owns land or other means of production in order to acquire the means that permit subsistence. Labour is just another commodity. With a basic income, workers would gain bargaining power *vis-à-vis* the employer since the financial security held out by a guaranteed basic income could lessen the pressure on workers to accept jobs under more or less abusive conditions. Leaving the job market becomes a viable option, which would give rise to a position of resistance that is much stronger than workers have now. If one knows that one's subsistence depends, directly or indirectly, on the person with the whip hand on the other side of the table, one's bargaining power is very weak.

In poor countries in particular this possibility of different kinds of non-dominated organisation of labour power could help to articulate alternative networks of production and distribution that would have beneficial effects in considerably raising levels of development and social and economic independence, while also protecting traditional ways of life. For example, a group of small farmers could buy buffalos or a tractor to increase their food production, and a truck to take their produce to a market. This would expand productive networks and reinforce sustainable community development, which would then give communities a more effective voice in claiming essential or improved infrastructure, for example schools, clinics, roads and bridges. In a post-conflict situation, like that in East Timor, a basic income would also have less quantifiable beneficial social effects in enabling a return to traditional forms of production, which require a close-knit community, and would help to defuse the potential for violence that flares up periodically and dramatically among disaffected, uprooted young people who have no opportunities to work, or because evident signs of increasing social inequality in such a traumatised society are a permanent flashpoint for ever-burgeoning frustrations and a generalised feeling of injustice. Creating the conditions of food security is of vital importance. Such a basic matter as a well-balanced diet could be greatly favoured, for example, if it were possible for people to transport vegetables to the coast and fish to inland villages. This alone could make a notable difference in the overall health of the population. Economic development is better achieved by breaking ties of dependency and promoting the emergence of robust productive projects at both the individual and group levels, projects that are autonomously conceived and planned from within the society as opposed to the often drastically inappropriate schemes that are imposed from outside or above.

Basic income is not especially difficult to finance. Each zone and country is different but it basically entails changing budgetary priorities, closer monitoring of the financial transactions of the rich, thoroughgoing reform of taxation systems or increasing VAT and excise duties on luxury goods such as cars, alcohol or tobacco to provide a basic income for all citizens and thus achieve a substantial reduction in inequality of income distribution and greater simplicity and internal coherence in the taxation and social benefits systems. The idea of the tax adjustments is that, even while the rich receive the basic income because it is universal and unconditional they also bear part of the cost of benefiting the poor by paying higher taxes.

Most countries show a stark contrast between a crude, socially polarising capitalist model, on the one hand, and the democratic values enshrined in their fundamental legal frameworks which uphold the basic principles of democratic citizenship and freedom, on the other hand. Basic income is far from being a panacea that would solve all the world's social and economic problems, but it would certainly start to bridge the gap. It would offer much more widely spread opportunities for people to participate in productive activities, enhanced social inclusion within reinforced local communities, greater political and social participation, and a major reduction of poverty and poverty-related problems. The material independence a basic income would confer upon citizens would expand their options for leading free and autonomous lives as individuals and as community members, and would nurture freedom, thus providing a basis for claiming and practising real, effective universal human rights.

Basic income is a new form of an old idea going at least as far back as the widows' estovers established in the Magna Carta around 1217, whereby a widow had the right to "her reasonable estover of common", her autonomous means of existence. Gerrard Winstanley wrote in the "Levellers' Advanced Standard" (1652) that, "True freedom lies where a man receives his nourishment and preservation". More than three hundred years later, the International Covenant on Economic, Social and Cultural Rights (1976) declared (Article 1 (2)) that "In no case may a people be deprived of its own means of subsistence". In the Monterrey Declaration, basic income is an institutionally guaranteed, inclusive and egalitarian form of property that might also be seen as one kind of indemnification of past and present wrongs because, in identifying basic income as a feasible institutional guarantee of the essential right of material existence, the Declaration calls upon the more privileged citizens to contribute, through tax reforms, towards achieving this right for everyone. Thomas Paine, in his pamphlet "Agrarian Justice" (1795 – 1796),[226] recommended the establishment of "a national fund, out of which there shall be paid to every person, when arrived at the age of twenty-one years, the sum of fifteen pounds sterling, as a compensation in part, for the loss of his or her natural inheritance, by the introduction of the system of landed property", after which he concluded, "It is not charity but a right, not bounty but justice, that I am pleading for".

If we take a condensed list of the human rights that are enshrined in declarations and covenants and supposedly for everybody, it is really depressing to see, even at a quick glance, how meagre their distribution is. What percentage of the world's population can say, "Yes, I enjoy all (or even a few of) those rights"? The list includes:

[G]eneral freedom; dignity; life; liberty; security; equality before the law; fair and public hearings by independent and impartial tribunals; presumption of innocence until proven guilty; freedom of movement and residence; right to seek and gain asylum from persecution; right to a nationality; the right to marry and have a family; right to own property; freedom of thought, conscience and religion; freedom of opinion and expression; freedom of peaceful assembly and association; the right to participate in government; the right to social security; the right to work by free choice and to have protection against unemployment; the right to equal pay for equal work; the right to rest and leisure; the right to an adequate standard of living, including food, clothing, housing and medical care and necessary social services, and the right to security in the event of unemployment, sickness, disability, widowhood, old age; the right to education; the right to participate in the community and to enjoy the arts and to share in scientific advancement and its benefits; the right to the protection of the moral and material interests resulting from any scientific, literary or artistic production of which [one] is the author. Additionally, people enjoy freedom from slavery or servitude; torture or cruel, inhuman or degrading treatment or punishment; discrimination; arbitrary arrest, detention, or exile; arbitrary interference with privacy; among many others.[227]

Mohamed Bouazizi and all the people who are now claiming their rights are yet again making it "plain that the world has long since dreamed of something of which it needs only to become conscious for it to possess it in reality."[228] May many more claim their rights and those of our fellow humans who don't have the voice to do so. The abstract nature of rights is, in reality, all too material because their situation has essentially been imposed from the domain of political economy. It is a question of taking the human rights declarations at their word and showing up the conflicts between different levels of legality, which basically boils down to property law versus human rights law and principles and, in doing so, reshape the world in the name of justice.

Given the lamentable state of human rights practice in the world it's surprising, perhaps, to find that several states of the United States of America, including Kentucky, Pennsylvania, Tennessee, North Carolina and Texas, enshrine the Right (and even duty) of Revolution in their Constitutions. The Bill of Rights of the New Hampshire Constitution (effective as of 2 June 1784)[229] states in Article 10 ("Right of Revolution") that:

Government being instituted for the common benefit, protection, and security, of the whole community, and not for the private interest or emolument of any one man, family, or class of men; therefore, whenever the ends of government are perverted, and public liberty manifestly endangered, and all other means of redress are ineffectual, the people may, and of right ought to reform the old, or establish a new government. The doctrine of nonresistance against arbitrary power, and oppression, is absurd, slavish, and destructive of the good and happiness of mankind.

Again, the *Grundgesetz*, the constitutional law of Germany (formally approved in 1949) recognises in Article 20 (4) that, "All Germans shall have the right to resist any person seeking to abolish this constitutional order, if no other remedy is available".[230] We have come to this: there is no "other remedy" or institutional effort to counter the erosion of constitutional rights. The task is to fashion a world where the human rights enshrined in constitutions and declarations are transformed into a universal reality. Surely unity based on a common upholding of principles of justice has to be stronger than the veneer of unity deriving from submission to centralised authority. People in many parts of the world are starting to construct what Hakim Bey (a.k.a. Peter Lamborn Wilson) called the "temporary autonomous zone". Let us make many, evermore autonomous and ever-less temporary zones, human rights republics that will keep spreading and spreading until we can truly talk of universal human rights.

The Universal Declaration of Human Rights is not mistaken when in Article 1 it stresses the fact that human beings are "endowed with reason and conscience". If we don't have universal human rights, human "reason and conscience" are empty words but we should never forget that "reason and conscience" can be our strength because, with them, "We have it in our power to begin the world over again".[231]

Footnotes

1. The Byelorussian Soviet Socialist Republic, Czechoslovakia, Poland, Saudi Arabia, South Africa, the Soviet Union, the Ukrainian Soviet Socialist Republic, and Yugoslavia abstained. The case of the Vatican, with its obstinate view that Church doctrine is above human rights even while it claims to be a State, is revealing with regard to non-signatories of human rights accords as it has only signed two of the UN's nine core human rights conventions, which is to say significantly fewer than China, Iran and Rwanda. The human rights lawyer, Geoffrey Roberson, has called for an end to this legal immunity, in particular with regard to priestly abuse of children, rightly insisting that the "Holy See can no longer ignore international law, which now counts the widespread or systematic sexual abuse of children as a crime against humanity". See Geoffrey Robertson, (2010) "Put the Pope in the Dock", *The Guardian*, 2 April, available from: http://www.guardian.co.uk/com mentisfree/libertycentral/2010/apr/02/pope-legal-immunity -international-law (accessed 15 November 2012).

2. Available from: http://www.un.org/en/documents/udhr /index.shtml (accessed 15 November 2012).

3. Elisabetta Povoledo and Doreen Carvajal (2012), "Increasingly in Europe, Suicides 'by Economic Crisis'", *The New York Times*, 14 April.

4. Karl Marx and Friedrich Engels (1848) "The Manifesto of the Communist Party", available from: http://www. marxists.org/archive/marx/works/1848/communist-mani festo/ch01.htm (accessed 15 November 2012).

5. Cited by Max Rodenbeck (2011) "Volcano of Rage", *New York Review of Books*, 24 March.

6. Available from: http://www.icc-cpi.int/NR/rdonlyres/0D802

4D3-87EA-4E6A-8A27-05B987C38689/0/RomeStatutEng.pdf (accessed 10 November 2012).

7. Ernst Bloch (1987) *Natural Law and Human Dignity*, The MIT Press, p. 153-4.

8. Mark Danner (1997) "America and the Bosnia Genocide", *The New York Review of Books*, 4 December.

9. William Shakespeare (c. 1610) *The Tempest*, Act IV, Scene 1, available from http://shakespeare.mit.edu/tempest/full.html (accessed 12 September 2012).

10. Grace Livingstone (2012) "The Real Hunger Games: How Banks Gamble on Food Prices – and the Poor Lose Out", *The Independent*, 1 April, available from: http://www.independent.co.uk/news/world/politics/the-real-hunger-games-how-banks-gamble-on-food-prices—and-the-poor-lose-out-7606263.html (accessed 4 November 2012).

11. Juan José Millás (2012) "Un cañón en el culo", *El País*, 14 August [author's translation].

12. Don Winslow (2010) *Savages*, London, William Heinemann, p. 131.

13. Raoul Peck's film *Lumumba* (2000), detailing this story, can be watched on YouTube: http://www.youtube.com/watch?v=IrbCOol_VVE (accessed 12 September 2012).

14. Available from: http://www.un.org/News/dh/latest/drcongo.htm (accessed 16 November 2012).

15. Fred Pearce (2012) *The Landgrabbers: The New Fight over Who Owns the Earth*, London, Eden Project Books, p.225. This book offers a chilling overview of the environmental, political economic, social and ethical dimensions of the drama of the global-scale land grab.

16. Available from: http://www.cnv.org.kh/personInfo/biography_of_hun_sen.htm (accessed 10 September 2012).

17. Quoted by Adrian Levy and Cathy Scott-Clark (2008) "Country for Sale", *The Guardian*, 26 April.

18. See Elizabeth Brundige et al. (2004) *Indonesian Human Rights*

Abuses in West Papua: Application of the Law of Genocide to the History of Indonesian Control, Allard K. Lowenstein International Human Rights Clinic, Yale Law School, available from: http://www.law.yale.edu/documents/pdf/int ellectual_life/west_papua_final_report.pdf (accessed 10 August 2012).

19. St. Augustine (early fifth century) *The City of God*, Chapter XV, available from: http://www.newadvent.org/fathers /120119.htm (accessed 10 August 2012).

20. Sarah Leo (2012) "Infographic: Trading at the Speed of Light", *The Bureau of Investigative Journal*, 16 September, available from: http://www.thebureauinvestigates.com/201 2/09/16/infographic-trading-at-the-speed-of-light/ (accessed 15 September 2012).

21. When the California Public Employees' Retirement System sued three bond-rating companies in July 2009 for losses caused by their "wildly inaccurate" risk assessments on three structured investment vehicles, Judge Richard Kramer ruled in San Francisco State Court that the false ratings by Moody's Investors Service Inc., Standard & Poor's and Fitch Ratings Ltd. in the $1 billion lawsuit are "protected speech". In other words, the rating agencies are protected by the "right of free speech", whatever the repercussions of their well-paid pronouncements might be. See "Judge Rules Bond Ratings are Protected Speech" (2010), 12 December, available from: http://www.moneynews.com/FinanceNews /bonds-fitch-s-P-moodys/2010/12/12/id/379703?KeepThis=tr ue&TB_iframe=true&height=808&width=1024&inlineId=m yOnPageContent (accessed 17 August 2012).

22. See Freedom House (2010) *Nations in Transit*, available from: http://www.freedomhouse.eu/index.php?option=com_cont ent&view=article&id=321:nations-in-transit-2010& catid=46:nations-in-transit&Itemid=121 (accessed 4 August 2012).

23. "World's Richest Woman Calls for Australians to Take a Pay Cut – 'because African workers are willing to earn just $2 a day'", *Mail OnLine* (2012) 5 September, available from: http://www.dailymail.co.uk/news/article-2198868/Gina-Rinehart-Worlds-richest-woman-calls-Australian-workers-paid-2-day.html (accessed 16 November 2012).

24. *World Bank Development Indicators* (2008). Caution is called for with the official figures. The usually-cited World Bank, scorning established poverty-measuring methodology, arbitrarily sets a "poverty threshold" of one dollar a day per capita, a statistical sleight of hand that reduces recorded poverty. Many population groups with per capita incomes of five dollars or more a day remain poverty stricken, which is to say unable to meet basic expenditures of food, clothing, shelter, health and education, and therefore to exercise their rights. Underlining the gross inequality embedded in notions of poverty, the film-maker Morgan Spurlock produced a television documentary series *30 Days: Minimum Wage* demonstrating that living on the minimum wage of $5.15 per hour for 30 days, earning $50 to $70 a day was, in the US, to experience great hardship.

25. United Nations Development Program (2007) *Human Development Report*, p. 25.

26. UNICEF (1999) *The State of the World's Children*.

27. UNICEF (2000) *Progress of Nations Report*.

28. George Kennan (1948) *U.S. State Department Policy Planning*, Study #23, February 24. (See also Foreign Relations of the United States 1948, Vol. 1, No. 2, 1976 for the full text where this was first published).

29. Maximilien Robespierre (2005) [24 April 1793] "Concerning the Declaration of the Rights of Man and of the Citizen". The following quotes from Robespierre come from a compendium of his speeches produced by Bosc, Gauthier and Wahnich (2005), available (in French) from: http://mem

bres.lycos.fr/discours/discours.htm (accessed 15 August 2012).

30. There are more slaves today than ever before in human history. In the words of the Slavery Convention, which came into force on 9 March 1927, "Slavery is the status or condition of a person over whom any or all of the powers attaching to the right of ownership are exercised". See also Skinner, E. Benjamin (2008) *A Crime So Monstrous: Face-to-Face with Modern-Day Slavery* (New York: Free Press).

31. Henry Shue (1980) *Basic Rights: Subsistence, Affluence and U.S. Foreign Policy* (New Jersey: Princeton University Press).

32. Jeanette Blom (2003) "Interview with Philosopher Thomas Pogge on the Fight against Poverty", *SHS Newsletter* 03 (UNESCO, Sector for Social and Human Sciences), October 2003.

33. James Baldwin (1992) "My Dungeon Shook" in *The Fire Next Time*, Vintage, first published 1963.

34. John Locke (1689) *Two Treatises on Government* 2, Chapter 5, "Property", paragraphs 26 and 27.

35. Ibid., paragraph 27 (emphasis added).

36. Ibid., paragraph 46.

37. Ibid., paragraph 47.

38. Ibid., paragraph 32.

39. "Substantive Issues Arising in the Implementation of the International Covenant on Economic, Social And Cultural Rights: General Comment 12, The Right to Adequate Food" available from: http://www.unhchr.ch/tbs/doc.nsf/0/3d027 58c707031d58025677f003b73b9 (accessed 6 November 2012).

40. Jean Ziegler (2008) *Report of the Special Rapporteur on the Right to Food*, A/HRC/7/5, para. 17, summary available from: http://www.righttofood.org/work-of-jean-ziegler-at-the-un/what-is-the-right-to-food/ (accessed 30 October 2012).

41. Ibid.

42. OHCHR (2007) Report of the United Nations High

Commissioner for Human Rights on the Scope and Content of the Relevant Human Rights Obligations Related to Equitable Access to Safe Drinking Water and Sanitation under International Human Rights Instruments. A/HRC/6/3, available from: http://daccess-dds-ny.un.org/doc/UNDOC /GEN/G07/136/55/PDF/G0713655.pdf?OpenElement (accessed 17 September 2012).

43. Full text available from: http://www.unhchr.ch/tbs/doc. nsf/0/a5458d1d1bbd713fc1256cc400389e94?Opendocument (accessed 24 September 2012).

44. Amnesty International (2009) *Troubled Waters – Palestinians Denied Fair Access to Water: Israel-Occupied Palestinian Territories*, available from: http://www.amnesty.org/en /library/asset/MDE15/027/2009/en/e9892ce4-7fba-469b-96b9-c1e1084c620c/mde150272009en.pdf (accessed 15 September 2012).

45. World Water Council website, available from: http://www. worldwatercouncil.org/index.php?id=23 (accessed 20 September 2012).

46. James Arvanitakis (2012) "The Biggest Mass Poisoning in History", *New Matilda*, available from: http://newmatild a.com/2012/10/15/biggest-mass-poisoning-history (accessed 12 October 2012).

47. For a more detailed account of the process summarised here, see William Engdahl, (2011) "Getting Used to Life without Food: Wall Street, BP, Bio-ethanol and the Death of Millions", *Global Research*, 3 July, available from: http://www.globalresearch.ca/getting-used-to-life-without-food/25483 (accessed 10 September 2012).

48. See OpenSecrets.org, "Agribusiness: Top Contributors to Federal Candidates, Parties and Outside Groups", available from: http://www.opensecrets.org/industries/contrib.php?i nd=A&cycle=2012 (accessed 6 September 2012).

49. Anthony Gucciardi (2012) USDA to Give Monsanto's GMO

Crops Special 'Speed Approval', available from: http://naturalsociety.com/usda-to-give-monsantos-new-gmo-crops-special-speedy-approval/#ixzz246SKosjv (accessed 12 September 2012).

50. See, for example, Brian Moench (2012) "Autism and Disappearing Bees: A Common Denominator?", *Common Dreams*, 2 April, available from: https://www.commondreams.org/view/2012/04/02 (accessed 21 September 2012).

51. Ibid.

52. Frederick Kaufman (2011) "How Goldman Sachs Created the Food Crisis", *Foreign Policy*, 27 April, available from: http://www.foreignpolicy.com/articles/2011/04/27/how_goldman_sachs_created_the_food_crisis?page=0,1 (accessed 13 August 2012).

53. See "Food for Thought", which offers a great deal of information, available from: http://www.scribd.com/doc/58850015/Food-for-Thought-Who-Controls-Our-Food (accessed 14 August 2012).

54. Albert Bozzo (2011) "The Economics of Food", *CNBC*, 26 April, available from: http://www.cnbc.com/id/42662144 (accessed 4 August 2012).

55. "US Government's Foreign Debt Hits Record $5.29 Trillion" (2012) PressTV, YoU.S Desk, August 18, available from: http://www.presstv.com/usdetail/256938.html (accessed 18 November 2012).

56. See Michael Klare (2009) *Rising Powers, Shrinking Planet. The New Geopolitics of Energy*, New York: Henry Holt and Company, for a sober account of depletion of energy reserves and the increasingly dangerous geopolitical situation in a world that seems set on a perversely destructive course.

57. Anthony Barnosky et al. (2011) "Has the Earth's Sixth Mass Extinction Already Arrived?", *Nature*, March.

58. Trucost (2010) "$2.2 Trillion in Environmental Damage

Wrought Annually by World's Wealthiest Companies, Contends UN Commissioned Study", available from: http://epoverviews.com/articles/visitor.php?keyword=Truco st (accessed 9 October 2012).
59. See Esther Vivas (2011) "Los porqués del hambre", *El País*, 30 July.
60. See Christine Parthemore (2011) "Rare Earth Woes Could Mean Trouble for U.S. Stealth Fleet", *Wired*, 11 May, available from: http://www.wired.com/dangerroom/2011/05/rare-earth-woes-could-mean-trouble-for-u-s-stealth-fleet/ (accessed 18 October 2012).
61. See, for example, George Monbiot (2012) "Must the Poor Go Hungry Just So the Rich Can Drive?", *The Guardian*, 13 August, available from: http://www.guardian.co.uk/commentisfree/2012/aug/13/poor-hungry-rich-drive-mo-farah-biofuels (accessed 13 August 2012).
62. Ibid.
63. World Watch Institute (2012) "Land Grabs" in Agriculture: Fairer Deals Needed to Ensure Opportunity for Locals", World Watch Institute, August 20, available from: http://www.worldwatch.org/node/8674 (accessed 12 September 2012).
64. Klaus Deininger and Derek Byerlee (2011) *Rising Global Interest in Farmland*, Washington, The World Bank, available from: http://siteresources.worldbank.org/INTARD/Resources/ESW_Sept7_final_final.pdf (accessed 4 August 2012).
65. Nancy Chau et al. (2012) "Contested Global Landscapes: Property, Governance, Economy and Livelihoods on the Ground", An ISS Theme Project Proposal, 15 February, available from: http://www.socialsciences.cornell.edu/1215/Geisler_and_Wolford_Contested_Global_Landscapes.pdf (accessed 11 September 2012).
66. See Adonis Diaries (2012) "Africa Land-Rush for multinational Agribusinesses", 9 June, available from: https://adonis

49.wordpress.com/2012/06/09/africa-land-rush-for-multina-tional-agribusinesses/ (accessed 10 October 2012); and the website "Share the World's Resources" available from: http://www.stwr.org/food-security-agriculture/land-grabbing-the-end-of-sustainable-agriculture.html (10 October 2012).

67. Margareta Pagano (2012) "Land Grab: The Race for the World's Farmland", *The Independent*, 3 May, available from: http://www.independent.co.uk/news/business/analysis-and-features/land-grab-the-race-for-the-worlds-farmland-1677852.html (accessed 15 September 2012).

68. Eric Goldschein (2011) "15 Outrageous Facts about the Bottled Water Industry", 27 October, available from: http://www.businessinsider.com/facts-bottled-water-industry-2011-10?op=1 (accessed 15 October 2012).

69. Jonathan Green (2012) "Tarmageddon: The Oil Firms behind the Exploitation of Canada's Wilderness Where Locals Say They Are Dying from Pollution", 9 June, available from: "http://www.dailymail.co.uk/home/mos live/article-2155344/Oil-firms-controversial-exploitation-Canadas-wilderness-locals-say-dying-pollution.html#ixzz2 3uuqOvRd (accessed 12 October 2012).

70. Liz Alden Wily (2012) "How African Governments Allow Farmers to be Pushed off their Land", *The Guardian*, 2 March.

71. Fred Pearce, op. cit., footnote 15, p. 11.

72. Liz Alden Wily (2011) *Accelerate Legal Recognition of Commons As Group-Owned Private Property to Limit Involuntary Land Loss by the Poor*, Policy Brief, International Land Coalition, March, available from: http://www.landcoalition.org/sites/default/files/publication/1006/2_PBs_commons.pdf (accessed 15 September 2012).

73. Human Rights Watch (2012), available online from: http://www.hrw.org/sites/default/files/reports/ethiopia0112

webwcover_0.pdf (accessed 19 November 2012).

74. See Fred Pearce, op. cit., footnote 15, especially Chapter 19, "Maasailand, Tanzania: The White People's Place".

75. Jennifer Franco and Sylvia Kay (2012) *The Global Water Grab: A Primer*, Transnational Institute, 13 March, available from: http://www.tni.org/primer/global-water-grab-primer (accessed 13 October 2012).

76. Ibid.

77. Ibid.

78. See, Neil Crowder, CEO Chayton Africa, Zambia Investment Forum (2011), available from: http://vimeo.com/38060966 (accessed 3 October 2012).

79. Grain (2012) "Squeezing Africa Dry: Behind Every Land Grab Is a Water Grab, 11 June, available from: http://www.grain.org/es/article/entries/4516-squeezing-africa-dry-behind-every-land-grab-is-a-water-grab (accessed 11 September 2012).

80. Fred Pearce, op. cit., footnote 15, p. 122 - 123.

81. Ibid., Chapter 3.

82. Ibid.

83. Ibid.

84. Available from: http://www.population-security.org/11-CH3.html (accessed 19 November 2012).

85. David Rothkopf (2008) *Superclass: The Global Power Elite and the World They Are Making*, Farrar, Straus and Giroux.

86. Rupert Neate (2012) "UK Investors Gather for Controversial Africa Land Summit", *The Guardian*, 26 June, available from: http://www.guardian.co.uk/business/2012/jun/26/uk-investors-africa-land-summit (accessed 4 September 2012).

87. Available from: http://landportal.info/landmatrix (accessed 23 September 2012).

88. Land Matrix (2012) "Transnational Land Deals for Agriculture in the Global South: Analytical Report based on the Land Matrix Database", available from: http://land

portal.info/landmatrix/get-the-picture#analytical-report (accessed 12 September 2012).

89. Franz Neumann (1966) *Behemoth: The Structure and Practice of National Socialism 1933-1944*, New York: Harper, pp. 20-21.

90. ECOSOR, U.N. CHR (2003) *The Right to Food*, 59th Sess., 35, U.N. Doc. /CN.4/2003/54 (2003) (prepared by Jean Ziegler).

91. "Memorandum by Mr Carne Ross, Independent Diplomat and former British diplomat, Select Committee on Economic Affairs", Minutes of Evidence (2006) July, available from: http://www.publications.parliament.uk/pa/ld200607/ldselect/ldeconaf/96/6071104.htm (accessed 4 November 2012).

92. Smita Narula (2006) "The Right to Food: Holding Global Actors Accountable under International Law", *Columbia Journal of Transnational Law*, Vol. 44, p. 29, available from: http://papers.ssrn.com/sol3/papers.cfm?abstract_id=951582 (accessed 10 October 2012).

93. *The Right to Food* (2002) G.A. Res. 56/155, U.N. GAOR, 56th Sess., Supp. No. 49, U.N. Doc. A/RES/56/155.

94. *The Right to Food* (2003) U.N. GAOR, 57th Sess., Supp. No. 49, U.N. Doc. A/RES/57/226.

95. Special Committee on the Charter of the United Nations and on the Strengthening of the Role of the Organization (2004) Working Paper: "Declaration on the Basic Conditions and Standard Criteria for the Introduction and Implementation of Sanctions and other Coercive Measures", parag. 14, U.N. Doc. A/AC.182/L.114/Rev.1/Annex I(14).

96. Narula, op. cit., footnote 92, p. 80.

97. Available from: http://www2.ohchr.org/english/law/cescr.htm (accessed 19 November 2012).

98. U.N. ECOSOC (1987) Sub-Comm. on Prevention of Discrimination & Prot. of Minorities, *The New International*

Economic Order and the Promotion of Human Rights: Report on the Right to Adequate Food as a Human Right, U.N. Doc. E/CN.4/Sub.2/1987/23 (July 7) (submitted by Asbjørn Eide).

99. See, UNDP (2000) *Human Development Report*, available from http://hdr.undp.org/en/reports/global/hdr2000/ (accessed 28 August 2012).

100. Albert Galvany (2012) "Sly Mouths and Silver Tongues: The Dynamics of Psychological Persuasion in Ancient China", *Extrême-Orient* 34, pp. 15-40.

101. Just Foreign Policy (2009) "Iraq Deaths", available from: http://www.justforeignpolicy.org/iraq (accessed 19 November 2012).

102. Cost of War, available from: http://costofwar.com/ (accessed 19 November 2012).

103. The White House (2011), available from: http://www.whitehouse.gov/blog/2011/05/02/osama-bin-laden-dead (accessed 19 November 2012).

104. Ken Auletta (2004) "Fortress Bush", *The New Yorker*, 19 January, p. 64.

105. In this regard, Obama is no slouch either. He has signed 138 at the time of writing. Information available from: http://1461days.blogspot.com.es/2009/01/current-list-of-president-obamas.html (accessed 15 September 2012).

106. Marco Aparicio and Gerardo Pisarello (2007) "Els drets humans i les seves garanties" in Jordi Bonet and Víctor M. Sánchez (eds.), *Els drets humans al segle XXI*, (Barcelona, Huygens), p. 135 [author's translation].

107. See for example this menu available from: http://www.tkrg.org/upload/fl_menu.pdf (accessed 3 September 2012).

108. Figures available from: http://iresearch.worldbank.org/PovcalNet/povDuplic.html (accessed 10 November 2012).

109. Thomas Pogge and Sanjay Reddy (2010) "How Not to Count the Poor", in J. Stiglitz. S. Anand and P. Segal (eds.) *Debates on the Measurement of Global Poverty*, Oxford: Oxford

University Press.

110. See also Sanjay G. Reddy (2008) "The World Bank's New Poverty Estimates – Digging Deeper into a Hole", available from: http://www.columbia.edu/~sr793/response. pdf (accessed 19 November 2012).

111. Thom Shanker and Eric Schmitt (2003) "A Nation at War: the Pentagon; Rumsfeld Says Iraq Is Collapsing, Lists 8 Objectives of War", *The New York Times*, 22 March.

112. Michael Hudson, a specialist in financial markets is eloquent on this point: "The economy has polarized to the point where the wealthiest 10% now own 85% of the nation's wealth. Never before have the bottom 90% been so highly indebted, so dependent on the wealthy. From their point of view, their power has exceeded that of any time in which economic statistics have been kept. You have to realize that what they're trying to do is to roll back the Enlightenment, roll back the moral philosophy and social values of classical political economy and its culmination in Progressive Era legislation, as well as the New Deal institutions. They're not trying to make the economy more equal, and they're not trying to share power. Their greed is (as Aristotle noted) infinite. So what you find to be a violation of traditional values is a re-assertion of pre-industrial, feudal values. The economy is being set back on the road to debt peonage. The Road to Serfdom is not government sponsorship of economic progress and rising living standards; it's the dismantling of government, the dissolution of regulatory agencies, to create a new feudal-type elite." See Michael Hudson (2008) "How the Chicago Boys Wrecked the Economy", interview by Mike Whitney, *Counterpunch*, 29 August, available from: http://www. counterpunch.org/whitney08292008.html (accessed 10 August 2012).

113. Cited in a US Department of State document shown in a

slideshow presented at the Joint CSIS. Woodrow Wilson Center Event on 20 October 2004 available from http://www.state.gov/s/crs/rls/37482.htm (accessed 6 September 2012).

114. Colin Powell (2001) "Remarks to National Foreign Policy Conference for Leaders of Nongovernmental Organizations", 26 October, available from http://www.yale.edu/lawweb/avalon/sept_11/powell_brief31.htm (accessed 10 August 2012).

115. See, for example, Jean Bricmont (2006) *Humanitarian Imperialism: Using Human Rights to Sell War*, New York: Monthly Review Press.

116. Cited in Naomi Klein (2005) "The Rise of Disaster Capitalism", *The Nation*, 2 May, available from http://www.thenation.com/doc/20050502/klein (23 July 2012).

117. Jeane J. Kirkpatrick (1981) "Establishing a Viable Human Rights Policy", paper given at a Human Rights conference at Kenyon College on 4 April. Cited by Bricmont (2006), op. cit., footnote 115.

118. Adopted by the United Nations General Assembly on 16 December 1966 and in force from 3 January 1976.

119. Adopted by the United Nations General Assembly on 16 December 1966 and in force since 23 March, 1976.

120. T. H. Marshall (1950) *Citizenship and Social Class and Other Essays*, Cambridge: Cambridge University Press.

121. Karel Vasak (1977) "Human Rights: A Thirty-Year Struggle: the Sustained Efforts to Give Force of Law to the Universal Declaration of Human Rights", *UNESCO Courier* 30:11 (Paris: United Nations Educational, Scientific, and Cultural Organization), November.

122. *El País*, 19 March 2008. This "very good situation" is one in which, at the time of writing, 1,200,000 civilians have died since the invasion, four and a half million people have had

to leave their homes, unemployment is at least 60%, some 40% of the population is below the threshold of "extreme poverty", and six million people survive thanks to humanitarian aid.

123. Amartya Sen (1999) *Development as Freedom*, New York: Random House, pp. 6-7.

124. Ibid.

125. This is expressed in the Preamble, *"Vida"*, of the Universal Declaration of Emergent Human Rights, presented at the Universal Forum of Cultures, Monterrey 2007.

126. Jaron Lanier (2010) *You Are Not a Gadget*, Knopf, cited by Michael Agger, "The Geek Freaks", *Slate* 3 January, available from http://www.slate.com/id/2239466/ (accessed 6 July 2012).

127. Zadie Smith (2010) "Generation Why?", *The New York Review of Books*, 25 November.

128. See for example, Sergio González Rodríguez (2012) *The Femicide Machine*, The MIT Press. In this book González analyses the unique urban conditions in which more than 5,000 women have been murdered, the terror tactics of narco-warfare on both sides of the Mexico-United States border, and the lethal blend of global capital, corrupt national politics and displaced transient labour.

129. Siyabulela Debedu (2012) "Justice a Long Way off for Dead Miners", *Inter Press Service*, 7 September, available from: http://www.ipsnews.net/2012/09/justice-a-long-way-off-for-dead-miners/ (accessed 25 September 2012).

130. Protos Onyango (2012) "Kenya's Water Wars Kill Scores", *Inter Press Service*, 11 September, available from: http://www.ipsnews.net/2012/09/kenyas-water-wars-kill-scores/ (accessed 25 September 2012).

131. Ed Pilkington (2012) "Bradley Manning's Treatment was Cruel and Inhuman, UN Torture Chief Rules", *The Guardian*, 12 March.

132. Nathan Fuller (2012) "Rule of Law Abandoned for Bradley Manning", *New Matilda*, 12 September, available from: http://newmatilda.com/2012/09/12/rule-law-abandons-bradley-manning (accessed 25 September 2012).

133. "Photographers in Los Angeles Considered Terrorists under Official LAPD Policy", *RT*, 7 September 2012, available from: http://rt.com/usa/news/lapd-suspicious-photo-sar-553/ (accessed 23 September 2012).

134. Abayomi Azikiwe (2012) "Africom Is Spreading Its Activity throughout the Continent", lecture given at the Adult Learning Institute, Oakland Community College Orchard Ridge Campus, Farmington Hills, Michigan, May 2, available from: http://www.informationclearinghouse.info/article32388.htm#.UErrnNp6KC0.twitter (accessed 24 September 2012).

135. Thomas C. Mountain (2012) "Bahrain Migraine for the USA", *Information Clearing House*, 8 September, available from: http://www.informationclearinghouse.info/article3238 9.htm#.UErrX6R3Bx0.twitter (accessed 26 September 2012).

136. Nazik Kabalo (2012) "The Call of Sudanese Women Human Rights Defenders, *openDemocracy*, 7 September, available from: http://www.opendemocracy.net/5050/nazik-kabalo/call-of-sudanese-women-human-rights-defenders (accessed 25 September 2012).

137. Hussein Abu Hussein (2012) "Rachel Corrie: Blaming the Victim", *Jadaliyya*, 5 September, available from: http://www.jadaliyya.com/pages/index/7225/rachel-corrie_blaming-the-victim (accessed 28 September 2012).

138. Ben Fenton (2003) "MacMillan backed Syria Assassination Plot", *The Guardian*, 27 September, available from: http://www.guardian.co.uk/politics/2003/sep/27/uk.syria1?CMP=t wt_gu (accessed 29 September 2012).

139. Available from: http://www.unodc.org/documents/data-and-analysis/Studies/Illicit_financial_flows_2011_web.pdf

(accessed 29 September 2012).

140. Rajeev Syal (2009) "Drug Money Saved Banks in Global Crisis, Claims UN Adviser", *The Guardian*, 13 December.

141. Peter Dale Scott (2012) "Why Americans Must End America's Self-Generating Wars", *Global Research*, 30 August, available from: http://www.globalresearch.ca/why-americans-must-end-americas-self-generating-wars/ (accessed 26 September 2012).

142. Ian Buruma (2010) "The Twisted Art of the Documentary", *The New York Review of Books*, 25 November, p.45.

143. Colin Turnbull (1984) *The Mountain People*, London: Triad/Paladin (first edition 1972).

144. Mike Davis (2006) *Planet of Slums*, Verso, p.199.

145. Ibid., p. 201.

146. Available from: http://www.unodc.org/documents/Global_Report_on_TIP.pdf (accessed 23 August 2012).

147. Pankaj Mishra (2012) *From the Ruins of Empire: The Revolt against the West and the Remaking of Asia*, London: Allen Lane, pp. 309-310.

148. Published by Breaking the Silence, Jerusalem and available from: jfjfp.com/?p=19918 (accessed 15 August 2012).

149. Available from: http://www.yale.edu/lawweb/avalon/un/unchart.htm (accessed 6 July 2012).

150. See the bibliography compiled by Amy Gilbert (2007) "Critical Texts on Justice and the Basis of Human Dignity", *The Hedgehog Review*, Fall 2007.

151. This is the gist of Martha Nussbaum's book *Frontiers of Justice: Disability, Nationality, Species Membership* (Cambridge, MA, Belknap, 2006), in which she addresses human dignity and justice from the "capabilities approach", a political account of moral entitlement. She is concerned with "what people are actually able to do and to be." (p. 70)

152. For example "dignity" appears more than a hundred times in the 1997 edition of the Catholic Catechism. Again, in the

Introduction, signed by President George W. Bush, to the National Security Strategy of the United States, we find the words, "Freedom is the non-negotiable demand of human dignity; the birthright of every person [...]", available from: http://www.whitehouse.gov/nsc/nss.html (accessed 15 July 2012). What President Bush meant by "human dignity" in such a document is anybody's guess.

153. John Lilburne (1648) "England's New Chains Discovered Or The serious apprehensions of a part of the People, in behalf of the Commonwealth; (being Presenters, Promoters, and Approvers of the Large Petition of September 11, 1648)", available from: http://www.constitution.org/lev/eng_lev_10.htm (accessed 12 August 2012).

154. For example, Jack Donnelly (2009) "Human Dignity and Human Rights", Swiss Initiative to Commemorate the 60th Anniversary of the UDHR, Protecting Dignity: An Agenda for Human Rights, Research Project On Human Dignity, p. 12, available from: http://www.udhr60.ch/report/donnelly-HumanDignity_0609.pdf (accessed 13 July 2012).

155. Thomas Paine would seem to be using the full meaning of *common*sense with his pamphlet of 1776 against British rule in America in which he defends the "rights of all Mankind" when he gives it the title *Common Sense*, available from: http://www.ushistory.org/paine/commonsense/ (accessed 10 August 2012).

156. Available from: http://history.hanover.edu/couam.htmlrses/excerpts/221h (accessed 8 July 2012).

157. As, for example, Pankaj Mishra, op. cit., footnote 147, has recently shown.

158. Gratian (ca. 1140) *Decretum*, Distinction I, *Ius naturale*, Ch. 7.

159. Henry Bracton (1976) *Of the Laws and Customs of England*, vol. 2, Belknap Press of Harvard University Press, p. 22.

160. Immanuel Kant (1784) "Answering the Question: What Is Enlightenment?", *Berlinische Monatsschrift*, December.

161. Check out this monstrosity, available from: http://www.
   forbes.com/2008/04/30/home-india-billion-forbeslife-
   cx_mw_0430realestate.html (accessed 16 July 2012).
162. Mike Davis, op. cit., footnote 144, p. 23.
163. Karl Marx and Friedrich Engels (1845) *The Holy Family*,
   available from http://www.marxists.org/archive/marx
   /works/1845/holy-family/ch06_3_b.htm (accessed 3 July
   2010).
164. Anatole France (1894) *Le Lys rouge*, Paris: Calmann-Lévy,
   Chapter 7.
165. According to the British Government in a writ issued in
   May 1792 in response to *The Rights of Man*.
166. Available from: http://infomotions.com/etexts/philosophy/
   1700-1799/paine-rights-399.htm (accessed 21 November
   2012).
167. Peter Linebaugh (2005) "Charters of Liberty in Black Face
   and White Face: Race, Slavery and the Commons" *Mute*, 23
   November, available from: http://www.metamute.org/en/
   Charters-of-Liberty-in-Black-Face-and-White-Face-Race-
   Slavery-and-the-Commons (accessed 4 July 2012).
168. Quoted by Linebaugh, ibid.
169. Available from: http://en.wikisource.org/wiki/Cast_off_the_
   Yoke_of_Bondage (accessed 12 August 2012).
170. Detailed by Peter Linebaugh (2003) "The Secret History of the
   Magna Carta", *Boston Review*, Summer issue, available from:
   http://bostonreview.net/BR28.3/linebaugh.html (accessed 14
   July 2012).
171. Ibid.
172. Peter Linebaugh (2008) *The Magna Carta Manifesto: Liberties
   and Commons for All*, University of California Press, p. 299,
   (Appendix offering a 1680 translation of *The Great Charter of
   the Forest*).
173. Jim Abrams (2011) "Obama, in Europe, Signs Patriot Act
   Extension", *San Francisco Chronicle*, 27 May, available from:

http://www.sfgate.com/cgi-bin/article.cgi?f=/n/a/2011/05/26/
national/w165822D43.DTL&tsp=1 (accessed 3 July 2012).
174. Thomas More (1516) *Utopia*, Book I, available from:
http://oregonstate.edu/instruct/phl302/texts/more/utopia-
I.html (accessed 9 October 2012).
175. George Orwell (1944) "On the Origins of Property in Land",
Tribune, 18 August, available from: http://www.coopera-
tiveindividualism.org/orwell-george_on-the-origins-of-
property-in-land-1944.html (accessed 21 November 2012).
176. Available from: http://ebooks.gutenberg.us/Renascence_Edi
tions/digger.html (accessed 12 October 2012).
177. This section on the "Large Petition" is based on Peter
Linebaugh's article (2002) "Levelling and 9/11"
Counterpunch, 7 September, available from: http://www.
counterpunch.org/linebaugh0907.html (accessed 23 October
2012). The online availability of the Petition itself (for
example at: http://www.bilderberg.org/land/petition.htm –
accessed 6 January December 2013) reveals an interesting
manoeuvre in the form of modern "intolerable mischiefs",
co-opting and once again turning things upside down, since
it is posted by such "naughty men" as members of the
powerful secret lobby the Bilderberg Group. The ultra-right
Mises Foundation has also embraced John Lilburne as "The
First English Libertarian" and offers the Petition on its
website (http://mises.org/daily/2861 – accessed 6 January
2013), with its very own interpretation of his importance as
a "liberal"(!).
178. This meant "justness" or right of property at the time.
179. Peter Linebaugh, op. cit., footnote 172, pp. 95-96.
180. Ibid., p. 101.
181. William Waterson, vicar of Winkfield, cited by Peter
Linebaugh, ibid., p. 100.
182. Ibid., pp. 102-103.
183. Ibid., p. 104.

184. Ibid., p. 112.
185. "Richard Parvin, Edward Elliot, Robert Kingshell, Henry Marshall, Edward Pink, John Pink And James Ansell: The "Waltham Blacks" Who Were Executed at Tyburn, 4th of December, 1723, for Murder and Deer-Stealing", available from: http://www.exclassics.com/newgate/ng169.htm (accessed 25 November 2012).
186. Available from: http://www.gutenberg.org/files/15399/15399-h/15399-h.htm (accessed 17 August 2012).
187. See "Slave Ship Zong (1781)", available from: http://www.hullwebs.co.uk/content/j-georgians/people/william-wilberforce/slaveship-zong.htm (accessed 17 August 2012).
187. Ibid.
188. Cited by NationMaster Encyclopedia, available from: http://www.nationmaster.com/encyclopedia/Zong-Massacre (accessed 29 July 2012).
189. Marcus Rediker (2007) *The Slave Ship*, Penguin Books, p. 40.
190. Cited by Eric Robert Taylor (2006) *If We Must Die: Shipboard Insurrections in the Era of the Atlantic Slave Trade (Antislavery, Abolition and the Atlantic World)*, Louisiana State University Press, p. 39.
191. See Rediker, op. cit., footnote 189, p. 138 – 139.
192. Charles Mackay (1852) *Memoirs of Extraordinary Popular Delusions and the Madness of Crowds*, Robson, Levey and Franklin, available from: http://www.gutenberg.org/files/24518/24518-h/dvi.html#page45 (accessed 3 August 2012).
193. Linebaugh, 2002, see footnote 177.
194. Alejandro Nadal (2011) "Derechos de las primeras naciones", *Sin permiso*, 23 January, available from: http://www.sinpermiso.info/textos/index.php?id=3873 (accessed 7 July 2012).
195. Available in English from: http://pdba.georgetown.edu/Constitutions/Ecuador/english08.html (accessed 19 August 2012).

196. Cited by Peter Linebaugh (2006, second edition), *The London Hanged: Crime and Civil Society in the Eighteenth Century*, Verso, p. 121.

197. Cited by Walden Bello (2011) "The Arab Revolutions and the Democratic Imagination", *CETRI*, 18 March, available from: http://www.cetri.be/spip.php?article2141&lang=en (accessed 18 August 2012).

198. Marx and Engels, op. cit, footnote 4.

199. Eugene O'Neill (1956) *Long Day's Journey into Night*, 2.2.

200. Karl Marx (1845) *Theses on Feuerbach*, available from: http://www.marxists.org/archive/marx/works/1845/theses/theses.htm (accessed 3 July 2012).

201. Adam Liptak (2008) "1 in 100 U.S. Adults behind Bars, New Study Says", *New York Times*, 28 February.

202. David Kaiser and Lovisa Stannow (2011) "Prison Rape and the Government", *New York Review of Books*, 24 March.

203. Marx and Engels, op. cit., footnote 4, Chapter II.

204. Rebecca Solnit (2010) "Covering Haiti: When Media Is the Disaster", *Guernica*, 21 January, available from: http://www.guernicamag.com/blog/1514/when_the_media_is_the/ (accessed 21 November 2012).

205. Cited by Rebecca Solnit (2005) "The Uses of Disaster: Bad Weather and Good Government", *Harpers*, October, available from: http://www.harpers.org/archive/2005/10/0080774 (accessed 21 November 2011).

206. Cited by Rogers Cadenhead (2005) "Police Trapped Thousands in New Orleans", *Workbench*, 9 September. The original interview is no longer available online from the *Washington Post*/UPI site, which is hardly surprising given the outcry after Lawson's comments.

207. See the History Commons website, available from: http://www.historycommons.org/entity.jsp?entity=travel_industry_association_of_america_1 (accessed 22 November 2012 – emphasis added).

208. Peter Linebaugh (2010) "All for One and One for All: Some Principles of the Commons", *Counterpunch*, 8-10 January, available from: http://www.counterpunch.org/linebaugh010 82010.html. (accessed 4 July 2012).

209. Kipling D. Williams (2011), "The Pain of Exclusion", *Scientific American Mind*, January-February, 30-37.

210. See Elizabeth Brundige et al., op. cit., footnote 18.

211. My thanks to Rezene Hagos for sharing his childhood memories of Asmara, Eritrea.

212. Linebaugh (2010) op. cit., footnote 208.

213. Ibid.

214. Kenneth Good, 2009, "The Drive for Participatory Democracy in 19 C Britain", *Commonwealth and Comparative Politics*, 47, 3, July, pp. 231-247.

215. Available from: http://www.usconstitution.net/xconst_Am1 .html. (accessed 19 July 2012).

216. Linebaugh (2010) op. cit., footnote 208.

217. Available from: http://www2.ohchr.org/english/law/crc.htm (accessed 22 November 2012).

218. Available from: http://www.un.org/esa/socdev/unpfii/en/ drip.html (accessed 12 September 2012).

219. Available from: http://www2.ohchr.org/english/law/ccpr. htm (accessed 12 September 2012).

220. Available from: http://www2.ohchr.org/english/law/cescr .htm (accessed 12 September 2012).

221. Adam Smith (1759) *The Theory of Moral Sentiments*, I.II. 28, available from: http://www.econlib.org/cgi-bin/search-books.pl?searchtype=BookSearchPara&id=smMS&query=di sposition+to+admire (accessed 8 August 2012).

222. Wilfried Hinsch and Markus Stepanians (2003) "Severe Poverty as a Human Rights Violation – Weak and Strong", Philosophy Seminar "Ethical and Human Rights Dimensions of Poverty" (UNESCO Poverty Project), All Souls College Oxford, March.

223. The following account of democratic republicanism and basic income, the mechanism it gives rise to as a minimal guarantee of basic freedoms, some degree of justice and guarantee of certain basic human rights on a universal basis has mainly been taken from Casassas, Raventós and Wark (2009) "The Right to Existence in Developing Countries: Basic Income and East Timor", *Basic Income Studies*, Vol. 4, Issue 2, August.

224. Available in Spanish and English from: http://www. idhc.org/esp/1241_ddhe.asp (accessed 12 July 2012).

225. For a full account of basic income, its functioning and its financing, see Daniel Raventós (2007) *Basic Income: The Material Conditions of Freedom*, London: Pluto Press.

226. Available from: http://www.cooperativeindividualism.org /paine_agrarianjustice_01.html (accessed 19 July 2012).

227. See the list compiled by Matthew Robinson (undated) "What is Social Justice", available from: http://www. pscj.appstate.edu/socialjustice/whatissocialjustice.html#_ftn 5 (accessed 22 November 2012).

228. Karl Marx (1843) Letter to Arnold Ruge, Kreuznach, September, available from http://www.marxists.org/archive/ marx/works/1843/letters/43_09-alt.htm (accessed 22 November 2012).

229. Available from: http://www.nh.gov/constitution/billofrights .html (accessed 21 August 2012).

230. Available from: https://www.btg-bestellservice.de/pdf /80201000.pdf (accessed 9 September 2012).

231. Thomas Paine (1776) op. cit., footnote 155.

Contemporary culture has eliminated both the concept of the public and the figure of the intellectual. Former public spaces – both physical and cultural – are now either derelict or colonized by advertising. A cretinous anti-intellectualism presides, cheerled by expensively educated hacks in the pay of multinational corporations who reassure their bored readers that there is no need to rouse themselves from their interpassive stupor. The informal censorship internalized and propagated by the cultural workers of late capitalism generates a banal conformity that the propaganda chiefs of Stalinism could only ever have dreamt of imposing. Zer0 Books knows that another kind of discourse – intellectual without being academic, popular without being populist – is not only possible: it is already flourishing, in the regions beyond the striplit malls of so-called mass media and the neurotically bureaucratic halls of the academy. Zer0 is committed to the idea of publishing as a making public of the intellectual. It is convinced that in the unthinking, blandly consensual culture in which we live, critical and engaged theoretical reflection is more important than ever before.